W9-ABW-022

CRAFT
cider

CRAFT
cider

How to Turn Apples into Alcohol

JEFF SMITH

The Countryman Press

A division of W. W. Norton & Company

Independent Publishers Since 1923

DALTON FREE PUBLIC LIBRARY
DALTON, MASSACHUSETTS 01226

Copyright © 2015 by Jeff Smith

All rights reserved. No part of this book may be reproduced
in any form or by any electronic or mechanical means
including information storage and retrieval systems without
permission in writing from the publisher, except by a
reviewer, who may quote brief passages.

The Countryman Press
www.countrymanpress.com

A division of W. W. Norton & Company, Inc.,
500 Fifth Avenue, New York, NY 10110
www.wwnorton.com

For information about special discounts for bulk purchases,
please contact W. W. Norton Special Sales at specialsales@
wwnorton.com or 800-233-4830.

Printed in The United States

Library of Congress Cataloging-in-Publication Data

Smith, Jeff, 1977 July 24–
Craft cider : how to turn apples into alcohol / Jeff Smith.
      pages cm
Includes bibliographical references and index.
ISBN 978-1-58157-313-8 (pbk.)
1. Cider. I. Title.

TP563.S65 2015
663'.63—dc23

                                    2015022601

10 9 8 7 6 5 4 3 2 1

OCT 05 2015

Bushwhacker Cider is, proudly, a mom-and-pop shop, and no one has been more of a supporter, friend, and ally than my wife, Erin. Pitching the idea of a cider bar to anyone else would have seemed crazy. Our company wouldn't be here if it wasn't for her love and support. So, for all the patience she shows me for all my dreams and ideas, this work is dedicated to her.

contents

introduction

IT'S SOMETIMES SAID that starting a business is the scariest thing a person can do in life. But for me, it may have been writing this book.

When we started Bushwhacker Cider in 2010, the venture was essentially born out of two things: a hobby gone mad, and the desire to be my own boss. But never did I think I'd be sitting in front of my laptop five years later, writing a book on cider. It's been a great experience, and one that has allowed me to share not only my own knowledge, but the wisdom I've picked up meeting tons of amazing people in the business – professionals and customers alike.

As I write this, we're three weeks in from opening our second cider pub in Portland. The great success of our first endeavor made me excited to expand, and to build a kitchen in which to explore food pairings and complete the experience for the customer. Our first location is a cozy pub and bottle shop, now housing over three-hundred bottles of cider from all over the world. We have eight dedicated cider-only taps, and we only carry four beers.

We've been fortunate to have been visited over the years by customers and producers from all over the world. At our tastings, I'm often the first geek in line to talk to a visiting cider maker. I've learned about cider cultures and techniques from British, Scottish, and even New Zealander cider ambassadors. That being said, I still get a thrill talking to a local home cider maker and hearing about the inventive ciders they've come up with. Sometimes I'm even lucky enough to be given a bottle.

Our second pub, Bushwhacker Woodlawn, is located in the northeast part of Portland and offers a completely different experience than our first pub. We offer a full menu, twelve cider-only taps, and a full liquor license; we can now start offering customers apple brandy, calvados, and the wonderful opportunity to explore the world of cider cocktails.

When designing the menu we kept cider in mind, of course, most – if not all – of the recipes incorporate our own cider or guest ciders.

Craft Cider, I hope, will be as informative and entertaining as a night in one of our establishments. Like our pubs, this book offers a unique look at the current market, as well as providing a history of cider and a few recipes I've put together to help you make good cider on a budget at home.

If you find me at one of our pubs holding a pint, feel free to let me know what you thought of this book – be it positive or negative. I've learned that being open to criticism is an important step toward my goal of making sure everything we do at Bushwhacker leaves you wanting to come back. Or in this case, to read more.

Cheers,

JEFF

CHAPTER
one

THE
WORLD OF
CIDER

When most of us think of cider, we often have visions of the Union Jack, fish & chips, and romantic, cozy cider shacks in the South West region of England.

BRITAIN HAS ALWAYS BEEN ASSOCIATED with cider, just as America is with apple pie.

While we're experiencing a strong resurgence in cider here in the US, England has been enjoying cider for over a thousand years. They have access to apples – and not just any apples, cider apples. It's a relatively easy beverage to make, and references to cider appeared in ancient Rome, in documents from the time of Charlemagne, and in first-century BC Spain. In fact, Spain takes credit for producing some of the world's first ciders, which is why, even now, they are respected the world over by cider enthusiasts. Orchards filled with traditional cider fruit have kept cider true to its roots.

• • •

Some fear that the growth of mass-produced cider will make these small producers, who continue to make cider in a traditional manner obsolete. But nothing could be further from the truth.

We find ourselves in an interesting era. New cideries are opening all the time, and the rush has even surprised lawmakers, who've changed outdated laws to reflect this "new" category.

There are a few big trends happening. The first – a rather controversial one – is breweries of all sizes getting into the cider business. Some see this as a bad thing, but I certainly don't. The most popular traditional-brewery cider comes from The Boston Beer Company, makers of Samuel Adams beer, with the ultimate find-it-everywhere cider: Angry Orchards.

Am I a fan of that particular cider? Not really. But I have a very dry palette. Do I think it's "good" for the category? Absolutely! Cider is now in about every store or bar in the country, thanks in part to the huge advertising budgets of big companies like Boston Beer with Angry Orchards, MillerCoors with both Crispin and Smith & Forge, and Anheuser-Busch with Johnny Appleseed.

Cider purists can argue until sunrise about whether this mass production is good or bad for cider, but the cold, hard fact is that it's here to stay. Whenever someone is buying a cider instead of another option, it's good for cider as a whole. These large companies know business, and those of us on the commercial side can learn a lot from them. Personally, I don't think they take anything away from "craft" cider makers.

We're also seeing a lot of smaller, local breweries making cider. Here in Oregon, Rogue, Hopworks, and Widmer Brothers have thrown their hats into the cider ring. It's cool to see them inspired by what we're doing, because god knows I have been inspired by all of them. Of course, the cynic says they're just in it for the money, but I disagree.

Another positive trend is the increase of quality in draft cider options. Draft cider has often been, and sometimes still is, considered an inferior product by cider traditionalists, who believe a true cider should come in a bottle or in the European style of a bag in a box.

Bag-in-a-box cider is just that; think of box wine. There is a bag inside of a box, and the cider is dispensed through a spout. Obviously the bag contains still cider, as a bag cannot hold carbonation. A few of these bag-in-a-box ciders make it over to the states, but most US cider drinkers don't like to drink still cider. I do, and there are a lot of cider geeks like me who do too, but the masses want some fizz.

I think the best way to drink cider is in a pint from the tap, and when we started Bushwhacker I certainly had my hopes set on crafting good draft cider. What's cool is that we're seeing high-end producers across the country beginning to keg their amazing ciders.

• • •

Cider was hugely popular in colonial America, and it was often used as payment to laborers, workers, and even professionals like lawyers and doctors! Oh the good ol' days. Cider, being a fermented beverage, was considered safer to drink than water, which was often polluted with nasty bacteria.

In the mid- to late-nineteenth century, as more Americans moved away from farms and into metropolitan areas, cider began to lose popularity. At this time, the waves of Germans coming to America started making beer, which obviously gained a great deal of popularity. Beer is cheaper and easier to make year-round, and it soon replaced cider as the nation's top alcoholic beverage.

For cider, the straw that broke the camel's back was the temperance movement. Temperance-happy farmers literally took axes to their orchards, cutting down the evil fruit trees that made the devil's drink.

Cider sat on the back burner for a long time in the US, until the early 1990s. In 1991, Woodchuck Cider, now the nation's largest cider producer, began their operations in Vermont. Much scorned by the "traditional" cider maker, Woodchuck has arguably done more to facilitate cider's rebirth and to keep cider alive in popular American culture than anyone else. The company started from humble beginnings, and they now crank out millions of cases every year. The massive company still supports and uses local orchards around their Middlebury, Vermont-based plant.

As the century came to a close, we started to see a new wave of traditional cider being made in the US. Folks like Farnum Hill, Alpenfire, Wandering Aengus, and AeppelTreow have been around for a long time now, and they're considered pioneers in the field.

When we opened in 2010, we – through no plan of our own – became the first cider pub in the United States. Our mission was to carry every cider we could, plus make our own batches. We were also Portland's first cidery, and one of only four in Oregon.

Flash forward to now, and Oregon has over twenty cideries, with more appearing all the time. The industry is now the fastest growing alcohol segment in the United States. Even in beer-centric Portland, cider commands four percent of the alcohol sold. That's massive!

People often ask me why cider has had such a resurgence. It's a hard question to answer. The easiest reply is because it's so darn tasty! But a lot of other factors helped.

For one, cider is naturally gluten free, and the gluten-free diet has become very popular over the last few years. I also think there's something very comforting about cider. Who didn't grow up drinking those little apple juice boxes? Third, cider is fairly easy to understand. You know what an apple tree looks like, you visualize smashing some apples into juice, and *boom*, magically you have booze!

Also, people always want to try something new, especially in a very open-minded alcohol city like Portland. And we like to get really geeky about it!

We're blessed in the Pacific Northwest to be surrounded by a massive amount of apples. Washington State even ships some of their apples to Woodchuck for their Granny Smith Cider! Though all varieties of apples can make cider, we're even seeing orchardists start to plant cider-specific varieties to help us get what we need in order to make more traditional ciders.

Over the years, several of us have coaxed these orchards into planting more varieties on a commercial scale. They were initially a bit worried, since they can't take them to market due to their extreme tannic flavor, and because these apples sell at a higher price. We've convinced them over the years, though, that if they grow cider apples, they'll have a line of cidermakers begging for every last windfall. So, now, hundreds of acres in the Northwest are being planted, and in a few years we may start seeing a lot of really new and interesting ciders come out, made from these locally-grown cider apples.

CHAPTER
two

STYLES
OF
CIDER

There could be, and likely will be,
some debate on this, but I think the styles
of cider available to us here in the States
are very distinct.

THE DISTINCTIONS AREN'T NECESSARILY GEOGRAPHIC, but are rather based on the varieties of apples used, the process of making the cider, and the types of additions.

English-style Cider

English-style ciders are made with English cider apples – no matter where the apples happen to be grown. An English cider has a mix of cider apples, creating a dry cider with a good amount of natural tannins.

Now seems like a good time to talk about tannins:

Tannins, in various strengths, are found in all apples. The tannic content exists in the skin of the apple. Cider apples are generally quite small, so that the pulp-to-skin ratio favors the skin. A massive Honeycrisp, on the other hand, where the flavor lies in the pulp, is a very low-tannin fruit. The tannins in a Red Delicious are relatively high among dessert fruit, but the inside is just a huge, watery sugar factory, so the tannic bomb is lost.

Tannins, in short, are what make your mouth dry out. The classic learning tool to teach people about tannins is to think of raw walnuts: just visualize what they do to your mouth.

Cider apples are chock full of tannins, and heavily tannic cider is a trademark of the English style. Besides using tannic apples, there are other ways to add tannins to your cider. Tannin powder is readily available at home-brew shops. The powder is extracted from grape seeds, chestnuts, and other substances. They do add tannin to your cider, and sometimes it's OK, but if you decide to use them I recommend a very light hand – no more than ⅛ teaspoon per gallon to start. I've tried some home batches that overused the powder, and it was not a pleasant drinking experience.

There are cider varieties that exist within the English category, as well.

Sweet English cider is available, which is actually created by adding fresh juice after fermentation, and not by adding sugar or other sweetening agents. Also, the English like to employ the use of barrels, both during fermentation and maturation, more than their American counterparts.

However, carbonation is not a clear way to define the English style, as some of the best English ciders I've had are still, which is not to be confused with flat.

Flat is a *fault*, still is a *choice*.

Additionally, most English traditionalists would never think of brewing hop ciders, cherry ciders, and the like. But I've seen this changing, as we've hosted a few English cider makers who took back with them fresh ideas to make cider appeal to a new audience. Still, traditional English cider drinkers, who often treat the words of CAMRA like gospel, turn their noses up at anything but a pure, orchard-focused product.

What is CAMRA?

CAMRA, or the Campaign for Real Ale, is a UK organization that, at its heart, has a great mission: to educate the public on what they deem to be a real ale, or cider, or perry. They even have a website that lists what is and is not a real cider. I look at the list sometimes and laugh, since most of the "unreal" ciders are also some of the most popular and well-loved! They list ciders that are "cold, fizzy keg products" as not real, which I have a problem with. And they look down on practices that spread the word of cider to the masses.

The reality is, cider would not be a booming business – especially in the US – if we had to be held to only making still, room-temp ciders. My own cider, which I go to an orchard and pick the apples for, and press by hand, and remove the sulfites from, and make with *love*, would not be considered "real" since I employ force carbonation.

I obviously have some strong opinions about this, and you certainly may argue with them. But, put simply, I think the narrow rules that CAMRA employs discredit a lot of-hard working people who make good cider that customers love.

In discussing CAMRA, I've been talking about smaller producers, and the ideal English cider. Obviously, in England there exist large-scale producers that we all know, like Blackthorn and Strongbow. Personal opinions aside, they have done a lot to provide cider consistently to the masses for a very long time. Do they have the same "traditional" taste as a West Country scrumpy? No, but even so their place and purpose in the market should be respected and appreciated.

Common English-style cider apples include:

- Kingston Black
- Foxwhelp
- Redstreak
- Brown Snout
- Dabinett
- Stoke Red
- Brown's Apple

Examples of English-style ciders available in the US:

- Oliver's Bittersweet Funk, made in Herfordshire, United Kingdom
- Henney's Dry, made in Herfordshire, United Kingdom
- Worley's, made in Somerset, United Kingdom
- Burrow Hill, made in Somerset, United Kingdom

US examples of English Style Cider:

- Farnum Hill, made in New Hampshire
- Alpenfire, (specifically their wonderful Pirate's Plank), made in Washington

Spanish-style Cider

One of the most surprising developments I've witnessed at Bushwhacker is how so many people have taken to Spanish-style cider. Being the grand master of funk, Spanish cider can be aggressive even for the most well-rounded consumer. I often describe it as the sour beer of the cider world – a concise description of a remarkable cider, made using the knowledge of generations of people who take their cider as seriously as their culture.

Though a few Americans have tried, it's very hard to copy Spanish-style cider perfectly. Basque and Asturian apples are rarely found outside Spain. And good luck finding the traditional maturation vessel used: a chestnut barrel. In the US, oak barrels are much more common.

While there are certainly nuances between different producers in Spain, they also share certain characteristics. Notes of olive and vinegar are intensified by the traditional high pour, adding natural carbonation and a bit of oxidation. Most Spanish ciders are still, though a few sparkling offerings can be found, and these can be quite wonderful. I liken them to a funky, light Champagne.

In my opinion, they lend themselves more to food pairings than any other cider category on earth. That's why we've added a Basque Cider Cocktail to our newest pub, in an attempt to spread the word about this tremendous cider.

While generally quite similar, there are some subtle differences between Basque and Asturian ciders. In my experience, Asturian ciders as a whole seem a bit lighter and not quite as bold as their Basque equivalents. The notes of olive on the nose are a bit more subdued, and Asturian ciders don't have as much of a vinegary ting.

Common Spanish apples:

- Errezila
- Geza Mina
- Goikoetxea
- Mokoa
- Ugarte
- Txalaka

Common Basque and Asturian Ciders Found in the US:

- Sarasola, from the Basque region of Spain
- Isastegi, (Basque)
- Castanon, (Asturias)

US Examples of Spanish-style Cider:

- Virtue's Sidre de Nava, made in Michigan
- Bushwhacker Cider's Txa Txa Txa, made in Oregon
- Troy 2013, made in California

French-style Cider

French-style cider is predominately made in the Normandy region of France, where they have their own kinds of apples, including bitter, bittersweet, and sharp varieties. These apples are rarely grown in large quantities outside the region, and this allows French cider to have a very distinctive flavor. The apples themselves are often quite small, due to the region's soil makeup.

A leading characteristic of French cider is the relatively low alcohol content – often between two and five percent alcohol by volume (ABV). This is due to a process called "keeving." While the science behind this process can be a bit daunting, the concept is quite simple: it's a way to make a naturally sweet cider, low in alcohol, by removing the nutrients from the juice. Eliminating the nutrients leaves nothing left for the yeast to convert into alcohol.

Most French producers also rely on natural fermentation, don't use sulfites, and refrain from adding extra sugar to sweeten the cider or boost the alcohol content.

Common Apples Used in French Cider:

- Judor
- Avrolles
- Biquet
- Muscadet
- Frequin
- Rambault
- Reine Des Pommes

Commercial Examples of French Cider:

- Etienne Dupont Cidre Bouché Brut de Normandie (E. Dupont Brut): Though more selections from E. Dupont can be found in the States, the Brut is the most commonly found. Made in Normandy.

- Eric Bordelet Tendre, made in Normandy

- Douche de Longueville, made in Normandy

- Louis de Lauriston, made in Normandy

US Examples of French-style Cider

- EZ Orchards, made in Oregon

While there may be a few smaller producers attempting to replicate the French style in the states, it's widely agreed that EZ Orchards, based just outside of Salem, Oregon, provides the best example of American-made, French-style cider. Kevin Zielinski is the owner and cider maker, and he's fortunate to have been born into an orchardist family. Over the past decade, he has cultivated an amazing selection of French apples in his beautiful orchard. His extreme attention to detail, paired with patience, makes his cider stand apart. EZ Orchard cider is highly regarded by customers, hobbyists, and pros alike.

American-style Cider

(or, if you like, New World-style Cider)

What's been going on in this country over the last few years has been pretty fun to watch. Experimentation is going full force, especially in the Pacific Northwest.

When we started Bushwhacker back in 2010, we could only get about forty ciders for our shop, and we had the basics of pear, apple, and berry ciders. But now the floodgates have opened, and we're seeing everything from ginger cider to our own Smoked Cider, a slew of hop ciders, and even ciders made with tea! Obviously, not all of the experiments work out. But it's a fun ride.

I define "American-style" as a catch-all category: ciders that don't feel constrained by the more "traditional" methods of production and apple sourcing. I've certainly argued with cider makers about this, as I feel it's important to find unique ways to use apples that are available locally instead of getting hung up on what makes a "good" cider apple. While we would all like to work with "cider" apples, it's not always a commercial reality.

I prefer to support local orchardists, to make sure their fruit finds a home instead of rotting on the ground. This, along with Americans' spunky attitude about doing things differently, has led to the vast array of new styles of cider you now see on the shelf.

That being said, it takes a careful balance to keep from turning these ciders into glorified wine coolers.

Commercial Examples of American-style Cider:
- Bushwhacker Smoked Cider, draft only, made in Oregon
- Seattle Basil Mint, draft and bottle, Pacific Northwest

- Reverend Nat's Hallelujah Hopricot, draft and bottle, Pacific Northwest
- Red Tank Lherry (lemon cherry cider), draft only, made in Oregon
- Crispin the Saint, bottle only, made in California
- Schilling Sriracha Lime, draft only, Pacific Northwest
- Finnriver Habanero, draft and bottle, Pacific Northwest

Cider is made all over the world, but most ciders fit into these categories. There are, however, a few minor styles I would like to touch on.

German Cider (apfelwein)

Germany has its own cider culture. Sadly, we don't get a lot of German cider in the states, so my own first-hand experience is limited. *Apfelwein* is generally a bit tart and sour. It also relies heavily on dessert apples instead of the classic "cider" apples used in other regions.

Possmann is the most common German cider found in the States. However, I've been told it's a very poor example, akin to mass-produced ciders found in other countries.

Irish Cider

Ireland produces cider, the most well known internationally being Magners. There are several new, smaller Irish producers, but unfortunately I haven't seen any of their ciders come through our fair shops.

Scandinavian Cider

Scandinavia produces quite a bit of cider. Rekorderlig and Kopparberg of Sweden are arguably the most popular. With flavors like "Strawberry-Lime," "Passionfruit," and "Elderflower & Lime," these ciders would definitely make the cider makers of South West England cringe. But they're hugely popular, and Kopparberg claims to have the "bestselling pear cider in the world."

Ice Cider

Ice Cider is quite popular in Quebec. Think of it as the cider world's answer to ice wine. Often sold in 375 milliliter bottles, it commands a fairly high price due to the complex process that goes into making it. Ice cider is made in two ways: either by freezing the fresh juice and separating the ice (water) from the juice, then fermenting, or by letting the apples freeze on the tree and then pressing the fruit while it's still partially frozen. *Brrr!*

The resulting product is quite sweet, and it's not something I usually reach for, but a good ice cider can be quite nice in small doses.

Pommeau

Pommeau is a mix of calvados (apple brandy) and fresh juice. The fresh juice cuts the high alcohol content of the Pommeau, and the mix is aged in oak barrels for a traditional twenty-four months.

Pommeau is a geographic designation; anything outside of France should be designated as an "apple dessert wine." We sell several pommeaux at our stores, and I really like them. They have the flavor of a fine brandy or calvados, without the immense heat that comes off most brandies.

CHAPTER
three

SOURCING
FRUIT &
JUICE

---

*Before we get into what equipment
and ingredients you'll need in order to
make cider, it seems prudent to talk
about sourcing fruit and juice.*

COMMON OPINION DICTATES THAT you need proper cider fruit to make "proper" cider. I've talked to hundreds of home cider makers who struggle to find such fruit, especially as the commercial demand increases. Here's a little secret: while cider fruit is amazing to work with, you do *not* need it to make cider. If you understand how to blend the apple varieties available in your area, you can make good cider without what purists call "proper" cider fruit. Supporting your local producers – your neighbors – outweighs sourcing fruit or juice from far away, in my opinion.

I'll get into tips for using dessert fruit (also called table fruit or hand fruit) later, but for now let me share some good ways to get the best fruit you can locally.

Farmers' Markets

Your local farmers' market can be a good spot to find locally grown apples and – more importantly – to create relationships with local orchardists. The key is to realize that orchardists bring their fruit to market to sell it as dessert apples for eating; therefore, they will expect and deserve a higher price – one that commercial cider makers won't usually want to pay. So orchardists likely won't want to negotiate with their prices at first. Talk to them about taking large quantities left over after the market is closed for the season or the day, and also be aware that you may be limited to what they have available at that time.

At the end of the day, orchardists are usually eager to avoid having to pack up a bunch of fruit and store it again. Be respectful of their craft, and you'll likely be rewarded.

Local Orchards

You can save a bundle if you go pick apples yourself, or with friends. I look forward every year to the fall, when I take employees out to the orchard to pick fruit for our house batches. It's so important to be connected to where your cider comes from – and it's also a lot of fun! If you're given free rein in the orchard, apple-picking is also the best way to have ultimate control over the quality of your fruit.

If you don't know where the orchards are in your area, ask your local home-brew shop. Or you can check online sites like Craigslist, or ask your grocer. Another good resource is your local farm extension office.

Make sure, before you start picking, to get clear instructions on where to pick, how to pick, and what's allowed in the orchard. For example, don't assume you can turn someone's orchard into a party spot, and bring lots of people with food and drink. If you do, it will probably be the last time you visit the orchard.

If you can get a sense of what's growing in your area, and what the season is, you may be able to do quite well for yourself if you pick near the end of the season. At that point, it's not usually worth the orchardist's money to hire a crew to pick for the last of the season. So you could get a screaming deal!

Also, look for "u-pick" orchards, and see when they close the orchard at the end of the season. I once got all the Pippins I could pick for ten cents a pound this way.

Grocery Stores

Grocery stores are useful if you don't have access to much else. They have their plusses: they stock apples year-round and they usually offer case discounts.

But they also have their minuses. Grocery store fruit almost always has a sticker on every apple, so that in itself makes it a pain in the rear to deal with. Also, grocery store apples are often large and can be troublesome to grind and press.

Some stores are willing to give deep discounts on apples that are almost ready to be tossed. For dessert fruit, the standards for appearance are high, so they often toss perfectly good apples for home cider making. I have found, however, that larger chain stores have strict rules about selling older fruit deemed "trash," due to liability issues. If your grocer says no, it's probably a rule they have to follow so they can keep their job, so try not to be too hard on them. If you can, stake out co-ops, smaller stores, and mom-and-pop shops. They will likely be eager to profit from unattractive fruit, rather than tossing it in the bin.

Juice

Sometimes you just gotta do what you gotta do.

Don't be turned off to cider making just because you can't find a good source of apples, or you don't have room to press them yourself. In the fall, it can be perfectly fine to locate a good source of locally made nonalcoholic cider. If you're lucky, you should be able to find unpasteurized cider, which is always preferred. However, unpasteurized cider can be hard to find thanks to some pretty strict rules about who can sell unpasteurized products. I know a few orchards that sell it here in Oregon, but don't assume unpasteurized cider will be common in all parts of the country.

Every book and every purist says not to use pasteurized cider, and to be fair, it does have its issues. But the fact is, you can use pasteurized juice and make perfectly drinkable cider. However, quality varies wildly, so don't expect amazing results with lackluster or additive-filled juice.

With that said, my first batch ever was made with my buddy Brian in my small apartment. I was nervous to invest a lot of money into this new hobby, so we made a batch from some low-quality store-bought juice. The resulting product was, expectedly, not the best in the world. But it was enough to sew the seed for me to take the next steps. So, if you want to get started, don't be scared to try whatever fruit or juice you have available.

The point to making cider at home is to have fun!

Neighbors

One of the Bushwhacker batches I'm most proud of was a very small batch I made a few years back from only neighborhood-sourced fruit. I literally went and knocked on doors that had visible fruit trees in the neighborhood around our pub. No one wanted money for it, and they were glad to see the apples go to a good use instead of falling and making a "mess."

Tons of people, even if you don't realize it, have apple trees on their property. In my experience, they're usually glad to have the fruit go to a good use. If you're super lucky, they may even have some "gross" inedible apples, and guess what those could be? Cider apples! Offer to drop off a bottle of your finished batch as a thank you, and obviously don't go trespassing or sneak picking. For an added trick, a cool experiment is to try wild fermentation, utilizing only the native yeasts on the apples to make a truly local batch.

City parks may also have apple trees you could use. I suggest talking to your local parks department, however, if you plan on getting a lot, and making sure you have permission. Since you're not doing it at this point to make money, it should be OK. But it's worth making sure.

What makes a cider apple different?

For a cider maker, getting to work with cider apples is similar to a woodworker having his choice of the most exotic woods. With a great selection of cider fruit, your job is simply to prevent something going wrong. It is indeed a treat and a pleasure to work with cider apples. Unfortunately, however, the amount of cider fruit available in large quantities to the home cider maker, or even to the commercial producer, is very low.

Cider apples, also know as spitters, usually have an amazing amount of tannin. They're quite small and, depending on the variety, can be quite finicky to grow.

Cider apples are generally broken down into a few categories:

Sweet: low acid, low tannin • **Bittersweet:** high tannin, low acid •
Sharp: low tannin, high acid • **Bitter sharp:** high tannin, high acid

When we talk about these categories we're almost always referring to European varieties, since most American varieties don't carry any of these characteristics in strength. Knowing these categories, and knowing what apples fit into them, is how a cider maker chooses his blend.

On the other hand, there are a few European varieties, like the Kingston Black and the Stoke Red, that make excellent single varietals. We carry two fine examples in our shop, brewed by the well-respected cider company Burrow Hill in Somerset, United Kingdom.

Volumes of books have been written on apples. There are *way* too many varieties to list here, but the rule of thumb is that you can indeed use any apple to make cider. The art of cider is in the blending, and experimentation is key to making interesting cider. Red Delicious with champagne yeast not doing it for ya? Try using an ale yeast, and dry oak it! Or do a wild ferment and add some honey for a cyser.

Play with it, and don't be afraid of making a "bad" batch.

Apples

Like I said before, I'm a big fan of being creative with what you have. Depending on where you live, your area dictates what you can find. That being said, there are some pretty easy-to-find apples available almost anywhere.

RED DELICIOUS: The most common apple in America, the Red Delicious, has a negative association among traditional cider makers. While it's true they don't have a large amount of complexity, they do offer some great aromatics. So they're useful in a blend. A cider made from one-hundred percent Red Delicious will likely disappoint you, but it can be a good base if you're going to add some strong other juice to it, such as a cherry or cranberry. This may also be a difficult apple to find cheap at an orchard, since most get packaged for the trade or sold at farmer's markets with no problem. Think of this as a good ten- to fifteen-percent addition to a blend.

Crab Apples

Crab apples are the cider maker's little secret, for many reasons.

Most people have no desire to deal with them, as they are small and labor-intensive to pick. Many orchardists have crab apple trees at the end of their rows for pollination purposes, and they usually don't see any value to them beyond that. They are tannic powerhouses, and a little goes a long way, but crab apples can turn a boring cider into a great one.

I personally love locally sourced Manchurian crab apples, from a great orchardist in Parkdale, Oregon, named Randy Kiyokawa. I pay a premium for these guys since I cannot make it out to pick them personally, and it's worth every dime. Our yearly batch of Le Grande Pomme – a little inside joke since the apples are the size of grapes – is one-hundred percent Manchurian Crabs, and easily one of my favorite ciders to make, and of course to drink!

They can be a bit tricky to grind and press, however. The trick is to have some bigger apples ready to go, and to toss them into the grinder at the same time. The yield is also not as high, due to their size, but I promise you'll get results that will keep you searching out these small wonders.

The best, if not the most practical, way to really see what certain apples can do is to ferment them separately and then do tasting and blending trials. Once you do your first press, you'll realize that the setup, cleaning, and teardown of the equipment is not really worth it just to try a few gallons. Unless you have ample room, it can be problematic to have four or five carboys going.

But if you have space and you don't mind the work, try getting several pounds of local apples and pressing them separately. Depending on your press and other revolving factors, plan on twenty to twenty-five pounds a gallon for your experiment. Also, keep in mind that yeast packs are commonly sold for a five gallon batch, so if you do anything smaller than four, remember to do the math and add less yeast.

Once the ferment is done, you can rack it off, and you should already be able to taste subtle differences between your vessels.

GOLDEN DELICIOUS: The state fruit of West Virginia, the Golden Delicious, is a very sweet apple, and it's easy to find. While it's fine to use for cider, again, this one goes best in a blend due to its sweet characteristics. Depending on how high you want your ABV and how sweet you want the blend, fifteen percent or so would be about ideal for a blend.

BRAEBURN: A nice sweet-and-tart apple, Braeburns are great to use in ciders. These apples have often been overlooked by traditional cider makers, but I'm starting to see them used a lot in West Coast blends, likely due to the Braeburn's nice acidity and low cost.

GRANNY SMITH: First grown in Australia, the Granny Smith has emerged as a really fun apple to use in cider. Do Granny Smiths add tartness and acidity? Sure, but some single varietals have started coming out, including our flagship Alice, made from one-hundred percent Oregon-grown Granny Smith apples. Granny Smith apples are grown in abundance, and easy to find from coast to coast.

This is a great example of an apple used in American-style ciders. Often ignored by "traditional" producers, this apple works both in blends and in single varietals. When made correctly, a single varietal Granny Smith cider has the familiar taste of the Granny Smith apples we all ate as kids.

A quick note: when I say an apple makes a great single varietal, I mean the apple itself carries enough characteristics to allow for a fully rounded experience.

JONAGOLD: Developed in 1953 at Cornell University in New York, the Jonagold is a great, flavorful cider apple that can be found at orchards for a good price. It's a cross between a Golden Delicious and a Jonathan, and it's used in blends by several commercial producers.

FUJI: A hugely popular Japanese apple, Fuji is the sweeter child of a Red Delicious and the lesser-known Ralls Janet. Fujis are acceptable for cider use, but employ them for sweetness and volume rather than for any distinct flavor.

GALA: A New Zealand-developed apple, Galas are a cross between a Red Delicious and a Kidd's Orange Red. Galas have a nice flavor, and they're easy to find year-round. Like the Red Delicious, they're great to add for aromatic qualities and juice yield.

HONEYCRISP: Honeycrisp apples have exploded in popularity over the last decade or so as dessert fruit. They're well known at markets for their softball size. So, are they good for cider? Like many other table-apple varieties, they're all right to put into a blend. But used alone they are very boring and, due to their usual size, a pain to grind. They also command a big price, usually in the two-dollar-a-pound category. With that said, not all Honeycrisp apples are big, and if you get to know an orchardist you might find Honeycrisps for a reasonable price.

NEWTOWN PIPPIN: An heirloom variety, the Newtown Pippin is quickly emerging as a popular single-varietal cider apple. Several commercial producers make a Newtown Pippin cider, and I've been impressed by all the ones I've tried.

It's well-known cider-nerd knowledge that George Washington and Thomas Jefferson both grew this apple variety, and Newtown Pippins have been around since the late seventeenth century.

ARKANSAS BLACK: Arkansas Black apples aren't exactly easy to find at most stores, but I bring them up because the trees are pretty easy to find at big box hardware stores. They're related to Winesap apples, and they have a very dark appearance when fully ripe. These apples are great for cider, adding a bit of tartness. Think of the Arkansas Black as a more interesting Red Delicious.

GRAVENSTEIN: An apple with a long history, originally from Denmark, the Gravenstein has become a very popular apple for cider makers. One reason is their early season: after a long winter, we're all anxious to start working with fresh fruit again! The emergence of single-varietal Gravenstein ciders has made this an even more sought-after apple. These are sweet, sharp apples, and they're often available from an orchardist for a good price.

Apple Math:

Ever wonder what a bushel is? Here are some facts to help you sort through the terms:

- **BUSHEL OF APPLES:** about 45 pounds
- **PECK OF APPLES:** about 12 pounds
- **TOTE OF APPLES:** about 650 pounds
- **KENNING OF APPLES:** half a bushel. Not used anymore, but fun trivia!

On average, one bushel equals about three gallons of juice – depending on your press and fruit selection, of course.

What's that tree grow?

- **DWARF TREE:** produces just shy of two bushels
- **SEMI DWARF TREE:** around five bushels
- **STANDARD TREE:** a whopping ten bushels!

A CIDER MAKER'S NECESSARY EQUIPMENT

As with any hobby, there are tons of equipment options out there for the home cider maker.

AND YOU CAN EASILY GET STRESSED out when viewing expensive apparatuses online or in your local home-brew shop. Here's my advice on what you need to get started.

SAMPLE SHOPPING LIST FOR YOUR FIRST BATCH OF CIDER:

- **2 five-gallon glass carboys**
- **1 siphon**
- **1 hydrometer**
- **4 bungs to fit the carboys**
- **4 airlocks**
- **One Step cleaning solution**
- **iodophor sanitizing solution**
- **1 yeast packet**
- **1 wine thief**
- **1 carboy cleaning brush**
- **1 funnel**

TO BUY AFTER YOUR CIDER IS READY TO BOTTLE:

- **3 cases of twelve-ounce bottles**
- **bottle caps**
- **bottling bucket**
- **bottle capper**
- **bottle "tree" for drying bottles**

Fermentation Vessel

The classic glass carboy does more than store pennies; it's actually the most common home cider choice for fermentation and maturation. Carboys are relatively cheap and easy to find, and they're fairly easy to clean.

If you do decide to get one, make sure you also buy a special brush that can be bent to clean the inside.

The drawbacks: they can be bulky to store while not in use, and they're obviously breakable. Plastic carboys have become more popular, and they're a good choice as well.

My pick? If you can find them, I really like plastic, bucket type fermenters. They come in many sizes and are very affordable, and they're easy to clean since you have complete access to the inside. I also like that, after they've been cleaned and dried, they're easy to stack and they take up very little space.

And they come in handy sizes, like the one I use the most, my thirty-liter fermenter. I also use them for cleaning small parts by filling them with cleaning or sanitizing solutions, and I've even been known to take them with me when I pick apples! Plus, they come in handy as stools when you turn them upside down. I'd like to see you try that with a carboy!

Barrels are another option, and one that is growing in popularity, as this method adds another layer of depth of flavor.

Sourcing and Using Wood Barrels

While they're likely impractical for most home cider makers, barrels can reap great rewards if you have the space, the ability to clean them, and the luck to source them. Here are a few tips I've picked up over the years. For our purposes, I'm referring to a full-size, fifty-one-gallon barrel. Smaller barrels are easily picked up at most home-brew stores, usually in five or ten gallon sizes.

SOURCING BARRELS: Brand new oak barrels are very expensive and – unless you're a serious hobbyist – probably best left alone. Also, a new oak barrel can have a very strong oak presence, possibly more than you really want. If a commercial cider maker uses a new barrel, they'll usually have a batch from an older barrel to blend the new batch with, in order to dial back the strong oak flavor.

Rather than using a new barrel, a better solution is to source an already used one. Local distilleries and wineries are excellent places to start. If you want to keep your cider one-hundred percent gluten free, avoid using anything that has had beer in it.

I've been very lucky to live in an area with many wineries and distilleries. White wine barrels don't do much for me, but several commercial makers use them often. However, red wine barrels can add some interesting flavor, plus some color, to a lighter cider.

My personal preference is to find used spirit barrels. I've had a lot of luck with rum, gin, and whiskey barrels over the years. If you look at the current marketplace, you can see how many more spirit barrel-aged ciders there are out there than wine barrel-aged varieties. A spirit barrel adds an intense flavor, one that I find compliments cider more than wine flavor does.

Commercial cider makers can sometimes get barrels for free. We often trade products for them and mention the donating company in our advertising for the cider. It's a win/win for both producers.

However, expect to be charged for used barrels. You'll likely pay around one or two hundred dollars a barrel. Remember, a winery or distillery is not a barrel store. So if you get a barrel from them, they're doing you a favor. Unless you create a good relationship with them, keep in mind you're probably on a long list of people wanting the barrels, including commercial producers in your area and others just wanting to cut them up for planters. Be cool, and you may just score a barrel. I'm usually on a wait list myself, since there are many other breweries and cider makers around that want the same barrels I do.

Also, you should know there's a season attached to wine, so don't walk into a winery at the beginning of harvest expecting to score a bunch of barrels! Wineries also use their barrels longer than a distiller, so don't be surprised to hear "no" a lot.

And finally, I would strongly encourage you NOT to get a barrel from "some dude." When you buy a barrel from a pro, you know it was properly stored and cared for. Otherwise, you run the risk of ruining an entire batch.

USING BARRELS: Ok, you got your hands on a cool-looking barrel. Now what?

A few things to keep in mind:

When not in use, you'll always want to keep the barrel hydrated. If you don't, the wood will dry out, and the barrel will fall apart. On a full-size barrel, you only need about ten gallons of water to do the trick. If you store it for a long time, make sure to occasionally add water, because you'll lose some over time.

When you first fill your barrel, either with cider or water, don't freak out if a little leaking occurs. Nine times out of ten, once the barrel is completely rehydrated, it will seal back up and the leaking will stop. Ask whoever you got the barrel from how it was stored, and when it was last used. They may suggest you rehydrate the barrel before use; in that case, you'll completely fill the barrel up with water for forty-eight to seventy-two hours.

The best-case scenario is: you get a barrel that's ready to go, and you have cider ready to mature or ferment in the barrel. If this is the case, you'll need to make sure you have your space ready. You'll also need to have your barrel rack in place. Barrel racks are steel racks that usually hold two barrels. They cost around a hundred bucks, and they allow the barrel to be stored above the floor, so you can easily spin it around to drain it after use. Home brew shops likely won't carry these, you'll need to go to a winery supply shop, order one online, or – if you're lucky – buy one from the same place you got your barrel from. If you're thinking about building something on your own, keep in mind the weight of a full barrel. Furthermore, according to some metal-working friends of mine, you likely won't save any money by making your own.

The barrel should be in a spot with easy access to water, a place where you can drain a lot of liquid. It's great if you have a pump to get nearly every last drop out, but if you're relying on a siphon instead, getting all the water or cider out will be tricky. At some point you'll want to spin the barrel and drain it; it could still hold a few gallons. In other words, make sure the space you've selected can get messy and wet!

When I get a barrel from a professional, I put my cider straight in, assuming it doesn't have to be rehydrated. I assume the barrel has been kept up – that it's ready to fill and always has been. But what do I do with the barrel once I'm done?

After the barrel's been drained and rinsed out, the easiest way to handle it is to burn a sulphur strip inside the barrel, with the barrel sealed up. This should kill all the nasty bacteria left over. But be warned – it's stinky! Most home brew shops with a bit of wine stuff may have sulphur strips, otherwise you get can them online pretty cheaply.

Once this is done, put in about ten gallons (no more) of water to keep hydrated during storage. Roll the barrel every two or three weeks, so the whole barrel stays hydrated.

When you get ready to use the barrel again, drain all the water, rinse, re-sulphur strip it, then fill it with cider.

Remember, even with all the best precautions and attention to detail, barrels are not perfect vessels. But if you decide to try a barrel out, and everything goes right, you'll likely be quite happy with the results.

Hydrometer

I know a lot of cider makers at home who've chosen not to get a hydrometer.

Can you make cider without one? Yes.

Should you? No.

There is no other way, short of sending your cider to a lab, to measure your ABV, or to know when fermentation is done. Hydrometers don't cost much, and they're super handy. One tip: make sure to buy a separate beaker for your hydrometer, instead of using the case they come in. Also, know that you will likely break it at some point. It just happens.

How do you use a hydrometer? Glad you asked!

To use it is to know it. A hydrometer measures the specific gravity of liquids – in our case, the measure of soluble solids and sugar in the cider. Water, for example, has a specific gravity of 1.000. The more solids, or sugars, the higher the number – and the higher the potential alcohol you'll get.

Hydrometers are calibrated to measure accurately at sixty degrees Fahrenheit. If your juice is above or below this temperature, you'll need to use the correction chart, commonly purchased with the tool or easily available online.

Take note of your initial measurement, and figure out what level the alcohol will be at if you go completely dry, measured at 1.000. To measure accurately, fill the beaker with cider from your batch. On a flat, level surface, fill until the hydrometer starts to float on its own. Spin it a bit to get rid of any bubbles, and to ensure that the hydrometer doesn't stick against the beaker. Take the reading, and note it.

When you stop fermentation, either at the point where the cider is completely dry or when you decide to rack the cider and stop fermentation, take your final reading. Subtract the numbers and multiply by 131, and this will give you your percentage of alcohol. For example, if your initial juice is 1.054, and you end at 1.000, your cider is about 7.074 ABV.

You can easily use an online calculator or an app to figure this out as well, compensating for any temperature difference above or below sixty degrees.

Wine Thief

A wine thief is a common tool that allows you to take a sample of juice easily, without disrupting the cider too much. You lower the thief into the juice and pull out a small sample for testing or tasting. I made cider for a long time without one, and this cheap tool has changed my life. It's the handiest way to taste your cider if you don't have a sampling valve – just make sure you sanitize the wine thief before sticking it into your cider.

Thermometer

The standard stick-it-on-the outside thermometer is cheap, but not super accurate. But it's fine for starting out, though you may want to get one with a probe for a more accurate reading. You'll also need one if you decide to use powdered yeast, to ensure you can bring the water to the proper temperature.

pH Meter and pH Strips

Most home cider makers, myself included, didn't start out working with a pH meter or pH strips. But I use a pH meter all the time now for commercial cider making, and I find it to be a useful and necessary tool. Monitoring pH levels is crucial for making sure your acid level is where you want it to be. With experience you can decide if you need to balance your acid levels by taste, but strips are cheap, and they'll ensure that you get better results. But make sure you get the right range of strips, as there are different ranges for different purposes. You'll want a narrow-range strip for cider, between 2.8 and 4.6 pH.

pH meters are cool too, but they cost a lot more, and you always have to make sure you're using the proper buffer solution and cleaning solutions. It really comes down to how precise you want to be for your home batches.

Airlocks and Bungs

I recommend owning at least two airlocks for every each vessel. They can break easily, and it's always nice to have some clean airlocks and bungs around for quick changes. Make sure to buy the right size bung for your vessel of choice. For example, one- and three-gallon carboys often have differently sized openings than a five gallon carboy. Airlocks are universal, but bungs are not. Buy an assortment and store them, because they will come in handy . . . usually on a Sunday when the home-brew shop is closed!

Cleaning Chemicals

An important rule: cleaning chemicals are not sanitizers, and sanitizers are not cleaning chemicals. You wouldn't wax your car before washing it, right?

There's a product on the market that I really like called "One Step." It claims it can be used as a single solution for both cleaning and sanitizing, but I always use a sanitizer after. One Step can be used to clean most of your equipment, except for kegs. It's easy to find at most any home-brew shop, and it's fairly affordable.

Remember, it's important with One Step, or with any product, to read the instructions, measure the product carefully, and pay close attention to temperature and contact time.

Sanitizer

I use a sanitizer called iodophor. It's an iodine-based sanitizer, and a little goes a long way. Again, it's very important to read the instructions included with the product, or with any other sanitizer. Like One Step, iodophor is very easy to find. And unlike other products on the market, iodophor doesn't have any of the common foaming issues that I've encountered with other products. But don't think that the more you use, the more you're sanitizing! Also, be aware that sanitizers in general use cold to slightly warm water, never hot.

Siphons

You'll need some sort of siphon to rack your cider. Auto-siphons work great and will do for the average home cider maker. If you decide to make bigger batches at some point, you can move up to a pump, but for anything less than fifty gallons a siphon will work fine.

Pumps are a whole other conversation. They can be very expensive, and though they're fun toys, a home cider maker will probably never need one.

When you go to clean your siphon, the easiest way is to completely submerge the tube, or better yet, to make a solution of cleanser and sanitizer and siphon the solution through it into an empty vessel.

Bottling Equipment

If you decide to bottle your cider, you'll need certain equipment. I'm assuming you don't want to invest a lot of money in a fancy, expensive counter-pressure bottler. For commercial purposes, purging the oxygen out of the bottle before filling is necessary to increase shelf stability, but for home purposes it's not needed.

The basics you'll need are: bottles of your own choice, bottle caps, a capper, and a bottling bucket.

I also suggest a bottle-drying rack. They tend to take up a bit of space when not in use, but are extremely handy for letting your bottles air-dry after they've ben sanitized.

You can also be savvy and use flip-top bottles, but make sure you completely sanitize and clean the areas around the seal of the cap. Also, you'll want to replace the whole cap after a few uses. I've received a few home-bottled gifts where I could visually see that the home cider maker did not take care to clean the cap. This lack of attention unfortunately ruined the cider inside.

Also, I would avoid using anything that has had questionable liquid in it, or anything with a screw top. However, feel free to reuse bottles in order to help save money. Ask your friends to save bottles for you as well.

Make sure you know the diameter of the bottles you're using, as there is a slight size discrepancy between Euro bottles and American-style bottles. Though the difference is slight, it's enough to matter. Both kinds of caps are available in home-brew stores, but make sure you have the right one on hand. Twenty-nine millimeter caps are usually for Euro style bottles, while the more common twenty-six millimeter fits American-style glassware.

I often read that bleach is OK to use for cleaning and sanitizing. And it is . . . but I still caution against it. For cleaning your bottles, I strongly recommend you use cleaners and sanitizers meant for home or commercial brewing. Bleach, if used incorrectly, can leave a detectible odor and taste in your final product. If you absolutely *must* use bleach, it's even more important to air-dry the bottles completely before filling them with the cider you worked so hard to make.

Kegging Equipment

If you decide to keg instead of bottle, you'll need some special equipment. For me, kegging at home was a changing point. Instead of sanitizing a bunch of little bottles, you only need to clean one keg. Also, I could try the cider from time to time in small amounts, without opening a whole bottle.

Yes, the money you would need to invest up front for the equipment is higher. Plus, you need to have access to hot water to keep the keg clean.

But if you have a kegerator and want to make the jump, kegging is a great way to go.

Let's talk about the keg itself. For home users, corny kegs, also known as soda kegs, are the way to go. They're easy to open, clean, and inspect. Plus, they're easily found through your local home-brew shop, or you can often locate a used one on Craigslist. They generally run from twenty-five to forty-five dollars apiece.

You'll also need to get a product called Powdered Brewery Wash, or PBW. It's relatively easy to find, and unlike other keg cleaning agents, which are packaged for commercial cider makers, PBW comes in smaller packages for home users. The big thing with this product is it needs hot water to work, and it requires at least thirty minutes of contact time with the container. After that, the container is rinsed with more hot water, and then the keg must be sanitized. So, if you don't have access to five gallons of hot water, kegging may not be for you.

You'll also want a kegerator of some sort, be it a store-bought one or an old-fashioned one made from an old fridge. Most home-brew shops sell kegging kits that come with the necessary hoses, regulator, and CO_2 tank.

It may seem overwhelming and feel like a lot of money at first, but once you're set up you'll only need minimal maintenance over the years, such as more CO_2, replacement gaskets, and upkeep of your cider lines.

If you decide to set up a kegerator but don't want to tackle it yourself, ask your favorite bar owners who cleans their beer and cider lines. Often, whoever does it for them will do some side work in this area, and they may be willing to help you out.

More About Kegging

After bottling your cider a few times, you may be interested in switching to kegging. Kegging offers some pros and cons.

PROS: With kegging, there's considerably less to clean and fill. If you're filling, say, a case of twelve-ounce bottles, with twenty-four to a case, you'll have to sanitize, fill, and cap all of those bottles individually, and they'll only hold just over two gallons of cider. Sure, it's fun for a while, but if you invest in some five-gallon kegs, you can fit a whole five-gallon carboy full of cider into one container! And you'll only have to clean that one vessel.

Drink what you want. Want to see how your batch is aging? Or maybe just want to drink a half pint before bed? Having a keg around allows you to test and enjoy as little as you want without opening up a whole bottle.

No bottle bombs. Maybe you have a batch that you added a bit of sugar to at the end, and maybe it decided to go into a secondary fermentation. With kegs, you don't risk having bottles explode— at best making a mess, and at worst causing injuries. Kegs can hold more pressure, and while it is possible for them to burst, it's unlikely.

Fill your own growlers. Once the keg is tapped, you can become your own growler-fill station, and take these larger jugs with you to parties, camping, or to the beach! Growlers also provide a neat way to pull off mini-batches and experiment with different flavors. Wonder what a cider made with those strawberries in your yard would taste like? Without sacrificing a whole batch, you can pull off a growler and go nuts!

When you fill a keg, you can force carb it, getting a consistent amount of carbonation into your cider without adding priming sugar, which is far less precise.

CONS: You'll have a higher initial cost. To start kegging, you'll need a kegerator of some sort, a CO_2 tank, a regulator, and a collection of hoses for pouring your cider. But these things will last a long time, and filling a CO_2 tank is pretty cheap. Most home brew stores will do it for you.

When you have bottles, it's easy to visualize how much of your batch you have left. But it's tough to judge how many pints you have left in a keg. It's no fun to be enjoying pints on a hot day and then bang, you blow your keg.

Kegs aren't perfect. You'll eventually need to replace certain parts, like the gaskets around the lid and the washers around the in-and-out heads.

Hot water is absolutely necessary for cleaning kegs. You'll also need special cleaning agents to make sure the kegs remain well-suited to holding cider. These cleaning agents (such as PBW) are only used for kegs and other stainless steel equipment, so they can't be used for bottles or other equipment you already have.

When not in use, kegs take up a lot more space than a few boxes of bottles. Also, you'll obviously need to have enough space to have a kegerator, or a repurposed refrigerator.

All in all, if you have the space and the means for the upfront cost, kegging is an excellent way to store and share your cider. Sure, the next guy may have a fancy label for his home brew bottles, but you, my friend, have your cider on draft!

CHAPTER
five

STEP BY STEP

OVERVIEW OF THE PROCESS

We'll go into further detail in a sec, but here's a quick overview of the basics of cider making, from start to finish. Look it over – you'll see that it's not that hard!

A Basic Overview of Making Cider

1. Start with a juice base. (see pages 78 to 81 for visuals) Take SpGr (specific gravity) readings and note them.

2. Add sulfites, if desired. Wait twenty-four hours before pitching the yeast if sulfites are added.

3. With your yeast of choice, following the package instructions, pitch the yeast into your vessel. To "pitch" the yeast is just a fancy way of saying to dump it in.

4. Attach a sanitized airlock, and fill the airlock with water. Try to keep the cider within the sixty to sixty-eight degree range if at all possible for fermentation.

5. In seventy-two hours or less, you should start to notice some cider goodness going on! The airlock will start bubbling away.

6. After you stop seeing visible signs of fermentation – likely at around seven to ten days – take a measurement and check your gravity. If it's 1.000 or below, the cider's done!

7. Using your clean and sanitized siphon, transfer the cider from your fermentation vessel to your maturation vessel. Attach a clean, sanitized airlock, and make sure it's topped off completely, either with other fermented cider, or with water.

8. For a basic cider, let the batch rest for at least one month, resisting the urge to open it up. Keep it in the darkest, coolest space you have.

9. Taste after a month, and see if it needs more time, or if you want to add any additions for flavor. If you take anything out, make sure to top off the vessel again.

10. When it tastes to your liking, bottle or keg the cider, and Enjoy!

This is also a good time to mention other resources to help you along. First, get to know the people at your local home-brew store. These days, they aren't just there to answer wine and beer questions; most are well-staffed with folks who have learned a lot about cider. Also, get in touch with local home-brew clubs, so you can bring samples by for people to try. As recently as five years ago, the "cider guy" was the black sheep at these meetings. But now, even the most staunch beer nerd is curious to learn about cider – and even to make it!

An In-Depth Look at the Process

So you've sourced your fruit, bought your equipment, and now you're itching to make some cider! Let's go. What follows is a basic method for making dry cider.

I'm going to start with the assumption that you have juice ready to ferment. Later on, I'll come back and discuss the steps to take if you've decided to buy fruit and press it yourself.

Before doing any of the following, make sure you've taken your specific gravity & pH readings.

1. OK, YOU HAVE FIVE GALLONS OF JUICE. The first decision to make is whether you're going to sulfite your cider. Purists avoid it, but it has its purposes. Sulfites will protect against certain types of infection, and they'll kill off any wild yeast in the juice.

I don't use sulfites personally, but I have in the past, and I don't have a strong opinion about them either way. If you bought pasteurized juice, you don't need to use sulfites. Also, if you want to take on the risks and rewards of attempting a wild fermentation, do not use sulfites. If you do decide to use sulfites, you'll want to have a pH meter or pH strips handy in order to add the right amount. Sulfites are sold in a few varieties, the most common being Campden tablets.

Dissolve the tablet in water before adding them to the juice, and go with the following measurements:

- **If your pH is above 3.8:**
  add malic acid before adding Campden tablets

- **If your pH is 3.5-3.8:**
  add three fifty-ppm Campden tablets

- **If your pH is 3.3-3.5:**
  add two fifty-ppm Campden tablets

- **If your pH is 3.0-3.3:**
  add one fifty-ppm Campden tablet

- **If your pH is below 3.0:**
  no need to add any sulfites

Sulfites, if added in too high a quantity, can give your finished cider a sulfur smell. You can sometimes lessen the odor if you pour the cider into a glass and let it open up.

2. **IF YOU SULFITE, WAIT TWENTY-FOUR HOURS** before adding your yeast. If you decided not to add sulfites, we're ready to go. Read the instructions on your chosen yeast carefully. If you chose a powdered yeast, you'll need to pitch it into the vessel before adding the juice. Typically, the packet holds enough for five gallons of juice, though it will work if you have slightly more or slightly less. Liquid yeasts are also available, and can usually be poured into the juice without pitching the yeast into the vessel first. Personally, I prefer liquid yeasts for their ease of use.

As I've mentioned, when I refer to "pitching" the yeast I simply mean the process of adding it to your unfermented juice or to the empty vessel before mixing the juice in.

Again, there's a lot of yeast on the market, made by a lot of different manufacturers, so read the directions carefully.

What yeast should you choose? That's entirely up to you. A lot of cider makers are doing great experiments with ale yeast, wine yeast, and of course wild yeast. You can get very geeky with yeast, even blending yeasts together when you feel confident enough to do so. I would one-hundred percent recommend using a straight cider yeast or a champagne yeast for your entry into cider making. Cider and champagne yeasts ferment very clean and add little or no flavor of their own. This way, you can rule out the yeast as the culprit if you get any "off" flavors in your finished cider.

3. YEAST SELECTION: Many commercial cider makers, including myself, experiment with yeast selection. The classic beginner's go-to yeast is a dry, or powdered, cider yeast. A very close second, if you can't find cider yeast, is champagne yeast.

Changing up the yeast is another factor you can experiment with to give your cider a unique twist. Some yeasts work better than others, and it's up to you to figure out what works well for the apples you're using in order to achieve the ultimate flavor you want.

I've had success, as have other cider makers, in using ale yeast. These yeast varieties will give you very different flavor profiles than traditional cider or wine yeasts.

Here are some solid yeast recommendations.

- Red Star Pasteur Champagne Yeast
- Red Star Côte des Blancs Wine Yeast
- Red Star Premier Cuvée Wine Yeast
- Red Star Montrachet Wine Yeast
- Lalvin ICV D-47 White Wine Yeast
- Lalvin 71B-1122 Narbonne White Wine Yeast
- Lalvin K1-V1116 Montpellier White Wine Yeast
- Lalvin EC-1118 Champagne Yeast
- Wyeast 4766 Cider Yeast
- Wyeast 4783 Sweet White Wine Yeast
- Wyeast 4767 Dry/Fortified Wine Yeast
- White Labs WLP715 Champagne Yeast
- White Labs WLP775 English Cider Yeast

4. **ADD THE YEAST, PER PACKET INSTRUCTIONS, TO YOUR BATCH. ONCE THE YEAST IS IN,** attach your sanitized airlock to the sanitized bung.
Fill with water until the inside piece floats, then attach the top.

Fermentation is ideal at around sixty-five degrees. The cider will ferment fine at slightly lower or higher temperatures, but any temperatures too far outside of this range will present problems. Closets, garages with cool floors, and other dark spaces are great spots for your cider. Avoid direct sunlight, or any place that's too hot or too cold.

5. **OK, SO YOUR YEAST IS IN THE JUICE,** and you know your pH level and specific gravity. Now it's time to wait. But don't think you can just sit back! You'll need to keep an eye on your batch over the next few days, especially when fermentation gets rolling. The airlock will likely fill with cider, and if it's a rigorous ferment it may get quite messy. I'd suggest putting a towel or rag underneath.

This is when having backup airlocks comes in handy. Have a clean and sanitized one ready to go, because you'll need to either pull and clean the current one or replace it with a clean one. You may have to do this several times.

6. **WHEN YOU START TO NOTICE THAT THE AIRLOCK** doesn't have to be cleaned as much, or that it has stopped bubbling, you'll want to recheck the juice with your hydrometer. Many home cider makers rely solely on the action of the airlock, but the hydrometer is an easy and accurate way to make sure the ferment is done. Feel free to taste the cider now, but don't be bummed if it doesn't taste perfect yet . . . you need to let the cider mature.

7. **MATURATION IS ONE OF THE KEY THINGS** that turns a good cider into a great cider. It's also incredibly hard to handle if, like me, you're an impatient person. When you begin making several, larger batches, it's easier to set some aside to age, but when you only have five gallons or so – and especially if it's your first time – waiting to enjoy your first hard-earned pint can be frustrating.

Maturing a cider lets it rest; it's a period when the remaining solids drop out of suspension to the bottom of the container to clarify the liquid naturally. If done right, maturation lets the flavor become more interesting. With most dessert fruit blends, three months is fine, though I wouldn't tell anyone if you let the cider mature for a shorter time. At least wait a month.

If you're lucky enough to get a higher-acid, tannic fruit, you'll want to extend the maturation time to at least five or six months.

Maturation is *very* important.

This is when you'll want to make sure the cider is in a cool, dark area. Preferably, store your cider out of site to help you resist the temptation to taste it often. When you're ready, rack it off using your siphon into a clean, sanitized vessel, making sure not to get any of the lees (spent apple bits/yeast/etc.) from the very bottom.

Also, the tube that goes into the maturation vessel should be placed as close to the bottom as possible, so as not to create unnecessary oxidation. Make sure the liquid fills the maturation container all the way to the top, using any cider you have to keep it topped off. Oxygen of any kind is not your friend during this time.

Now leave it alone! Forget about it if you can, and let it sit for a few weeks before even trying it. I know it's hard, but the more you open it and test it, the greater your risk of infecting the cider.

Some folks will want to rack it off again, to help further clarify the cider. I advocate you only rack it off once, and be patient. Give the cider time. Some commercial producers, especially the French, like to rack more than once, but most commercial producers have procedures in place to avoid any kind of infection. Bigger producers have bigger equipment to control the process. You likely will not have such procedures, so be careful.

8. ONCE THE DESIRED (at minimum, the suggested) amount of time has passed, it's time to put the cider into your package of choice, be it keg or bottle. Also, now is when you'll need to decide if you want a still or a carbonated cider.

9. **IF YOU PREFER A STILL CIDER,** you're almost done. Rack off into your bottling bucket. Have your clean, sanitized, and dry bottles ready to go, and make sure you have enough caps for the amount of bottles sanitized. Then, simply put a bottle under the spout, fill it, and cap it. I also recommend that you attach a clean tube to the spout on the bottling bucket that fits into your bottle, and fill from the bottom up. I enjoy still cider, and so do a lot of other people. But, the vast majority of cider drinkers want bubbles.

10. **THE OLD SCHOOL WAY TO CARBONATE** is known as bottle conditioning. This method works most of the time, but it can be tricky to get it right consistently. It can also be dangerous. This approach incorporates a bit of sugar inserted into the bottle just before it's capped, meaning some of the leftover live yeast will eat the sugar and create carbonation. The problem is, unless you're using heavyweight glass, the pressure could cause the bottle to explode.

11. **IF YOU KEG, YOU HAVE THE OPTION TO FORCE CARBONATE.** This is when you chill the cider to around thirty-five degrees, run CO_2 into it for forty-eight to seventy-two hours, and then force the CO_2 bubbles in, running the gas at a higher rate than you would to pour it.

Cider is normally poured at ten psi, but when you force carb you'll crank it up to thirty psi, so you'll have to make sure the cider is cold enough to accept the bubbles. After it's carbonated, you can simply serve it on tap, or you can set up a system to bottle off of the keg. This is the safest and most consistent way to carbonate, as you're not adding sugar and thus risking a bottle bomb.

SO YOU WANT TO PRESS YOUR OWN APPLES?

Nothing quite matches the satisfaction of pressing your own apples for cider.

YOU HAVE ULTIMATE CONTROL OVER the quality and blend of your apples, which will eventually end up in an amazing drink that you can enjoy with your friends and family.

I've already talked about where to get fruit and discussed what apples you can use. So now let's talk about how to go from apple to juice.

Presses

The first thing you need to do is figure out what kind of press you want to use or – more likely – what kind of press you're able to obtain.

The first step would be to see if your local shop rents apple presses, like our home-brew shops here in Portland do. If they do, they're likely to have the ol' standby: the screw press. Typically these presses have two baskets, so you can grind apples as you press. These presses are great to start with and usually cheap to rent, but the yield, of course, is not as great as with a professional press.

In my experience using one of these presses, you'll average twenty pounds or so to the gallon. Obviously, these number vary wildly with what kind of apple you use. But there are some tricks to make sure you get the most out the press and the apples you have:

1. A lot of home-brew shops are closed on Sundays. If you can swing it, rent the press on Saturday. Most places won't charge you for that Sunday, and you can get an extra day for free.

2. Planning for a quick four-hour press? Double it! Pressing apples takes a lot of work. Give yourself plenty of time to set up, press, and tear down. You'll want to make sure you return the press as squeaky clean as when you got it.

3. Rice hulls, a well-known secret to getting the most out of your pomace, are your friend. Almost all home-brew shops sell rice hulls, and they're super affordable. You simply mix them into your pomace, and they create little channels for the juice to travel better – without adding any flavor to your juice. Add about two cups per pressing-basket full, and mix in well. The drier the pomace, the more you'll want to use.

4. Don't sweat the small stuff . . . but sweat those apples! Sweating apples means letting them rest after they've been picked. When the apples are sweated at room temperature, it allows the moisture content to lessen and the sugars to increase. And as we know, more sugar equals more booze!

The rule of thumb is, they're done sweating when you can gently press your finger into an apple and it leaves an impression but still feels sound. But the reality is that if you're doing this in tight quarters, you may not have space to sweat your apples for very long. Ideally you want to sweat, but don't be discouraged if you can't. Sweating will also make the apples easier to grind, assuming your rented press, with grinder attached, is hand powered. For sweating, you'll want at least five days at room temperature.

If you rent a press, make sure you treat it like any other piece of brewing equipment you have. Make up a cleaning and sanitizing solution, and give it a thorough clean. I like to make a cleaning solution and clean the press well. Then I make up a sanitizing solution, put it into a spray bottle, and spray down the whole press, allowing it to air-dry.

The press you rent and start with will likely be a screw press, also known as a double-tub press. But this is definitely not the only kind of press out there. As with anything, it all comes down to how much money you want to spend, and how much volume you plan on pressing.

RACK-AND-CLOTH PRESS: The next step up for a serious home cider maker is a rack-and-cloth press. The basic idea here is the racks are filled with the pomace and made into "cheeses." Cheeses are layers of pomace that go into a cloth and are then folded together. The cheeses go into the racks, and the racks are stacked on top of each other. Once stacked, the press squeezes down from the top and the juice flows out.

Plans for rack-and-cloth presses to be made at home are all over the internet. I've never personally built one, but if you have the mechanical skills it would be a cool project!

I like these presses, but I personally like to use stainless steel whenever possible. Most of these are wood, unless you buy a commercially made one built with more metal. They're also quite bulky.

Still, being the classic press you see on farms and orchards, they do have a sense of romance about them.

BLADDER PRESS: This is what I use at Bushwhacker, and I've been really pleased with it. The bladder press is made with high-grade steel, and the idea is simple. The press contains a rubber bladder in the middle. You fill up the press with pomace while the bladder is empty. After you put the pomace into the press, you slowly start filling the bladder up with water. As the bladder fills, it presses against the pomace and juice comes flowing out.

Mine is on wheels and takes up very little space in my production area. The downside is that they're pretty spendy, and once the bladder fills, you need to dump all the water out between presses. I haven't come up with a clever way to reuse that water.

They do have smaller versions than mine (and much *much* bigger ones) that rely on filling the bladder with air instead of water. I haven't tried one, but for a home user they may be a great option.

BELT PRESSES AND ACCORDION PRESSES: Used mainly by commercial makers, these presses take up a substantial amount of room and can easily cost tens of thousands of dollars. You're free to drool over them, but I suspect you won't have one in your garage anytime soon.

Don't want to buy a press, or rent one?

Check with local orchards to see if they'll custom-press your fruit for you. They might be keen on making some money from a piece of equipment they only use for a short time each year.

Also, if you have any juice companies in your area, see if they want to press for you as well. Most of them have really nice presses with an awesome yield that you're not likely to get from your rented one.

So you picked out a press. Good for you! But how are you going to grind your apples?

The presses you rent will likely have a hand-driven grinder on them, or possibly a motor-driven one. Most presses, however, need some sort of external grinder to do that work for you.

There are plans online that show you how to build a grinder from an old garbage disposal, or even from a wood chipper! I say do what you're comfortable with. But I've also heard disaster stories about these grinders, since they're not made with the grade of steel needed for constant use with highly acidic products.

The only other option that makes sense, if you're very serious, is to invest in a stand-alone grinder made specifically for fruit. I've had mine for years now and had zero issues with it. But be prepared to spend at least fifteen-hundred dollars. You'll have to ask yourself if it's worth it.

You'll likely do just fine with the one attached to the press you bought or rented.

APPLES: You should wash your apples before pressing them, but *after* sweating them. Use only clean water, with nothing else in it. The bigger the basin you choose to do this in, the better. During this process, look for any apples that sink to the bottom. You do *not* want to use these; good apples float, bad ones sink. This is also an excellent chance to inspect all of your fruit. If you bought your apples at a store, make sure to get the pesky little stickers off of them before grinding them.

THE BAGS: You'll want to line your press of choice with some sort of straining bag, which you press through. These bags will also need to be cleaned and sanitized before use. Make sure, when you buy them, that they fit the press you've selected. If taken good care of, these bags should last you many, many years. Let them completely air-dry before putting them away until your next use. These are almost always available at the same home-brew shop where you rented the press.

PREPARING: Make sure you have all the buckets cleaned and sanitized before you start pressing. Also, make sure you know what size buckets you want to use, and that they fit under the spout. When the juice starts flowing it comes out fast. When you take a bucket away, make sure you pour it into your carboy so you have another bucket ready to go – you don't want to lose a single drop of your hard-earned cider. If you do use a separate grinder, you'll also need plenty of buckets to grind your pomace into.

Pull the apples from the water, and start loading up your grinder. Don't overload it; grind only a few handfuls at a time. If you're grinding small apples, such as crabs, make sure to have a few larger apples handy to throw into the mix. This will help the smaller apples go through the press. Fill up your bucket, and mix in some rice hulls if the pomace is particularly dry.

Transfer the pomace to your press. Fair warning: pressing is time consuming, labor intensive, and messy. Go slow. No matter what kind of press you have, you'll want to slowly add pressure and let the pomace do its thing. For example, in the typical rented press you'll find at home-brew stores, each press will take you at least thirty minutes.

I also recommend, once you think you've gotten every last drop out, that you undo the press, get in there with your hands, remix the pomace, and try another pressing to squeeze out every last ounce.

Well, now you have a problem I bet you didn't predict. . . . What do you do with all that dry pomace?

POMACE PROBLEMS: First of all, the most important thing is to figure out how you're going to get rid of your pomace *before* you start. Pomace has limited use. It doesn't compost well, and if you just throw it into your yard it can invite critters you may not want to attract.

That being said, I've heard of some clever ways to get rid of pomace, and I'll throw in some thoughts of my own:

Put an ad up online and let people now you'll have pomace available on a certain day. Some claim that pomace is great to add acid to the soil of certain plants that like it, such as blueberries. Whatever their reason, if they take it, it's gone!

Contact local farmers if you can. At Bushwhacker, we load up buckets of the stuff and give it to a guy who feeds his animals with it. Be warned though, if you plan on doing this for your own animals, they'll eat it until they get sick. I will say, though, from personal experience, chickens don't seem to like it as much as cows or pigs.

I've also heard some cool stories of people drying the pomace out and adding it to the wood as they smoke meats or fish. I've never tried it myself, but it sounds like a groovy idea.

Our friends at Reverend Nat's and Cider Riot! – both Portland-based cideries – use spent pomace to make a traditional ciderkin. A ciderkin is a very low-alcohol cider, made from adding water into the pomace after you finish with it, and then repressing it. If you do this, you're probably looking at a two- to three-percent ABV finished product. I've had theirs, and while it lacks immense complexity or body, it's one of the most refreshing drinks I've ever had!

If you come up with another way to use pomace, please drop me a line! I've always wondered if pomace could be used for baking or cooking.

Another note about pomace: make sure you wear your least-beloved clothes while you press. Pomace can permanently stain anything it touches, so put your fancy pants away!

A Basic Overview of Pressing Apples

(see pages 78 to 81 for visuals)

1. **PURCHASE APPLES FROM A STORE** or a local orchardist. When buying, think about the balance of flavors you want your final cider to have.

2. **WHEN THE APPLES ARE BACK HOME,** let them sweat to soften them up a little – usually five days or so, at room temperature.

3. **WHEN THE AROMA IS STRONG,** and the apples can be pushed in a bit with your thumb, wash the apples with regular water in as large a container as possible. Discard any apples that sink to the bottom of the tub. Also, remove any stickers affixed to the fruit.

4. **MAKE SURE YOU'VE CLEANED** and sanitized your grinder and press. Then place your sanitized buckets where they will catch your juice.

5. **LINE YOUR BASKET** under your hand grinder, or have your bucket ready beneath your electric one, so that it's ready to catch the pomace. Start putting apples into your grinder. If the grinder has a hand crank, I feel it's easier to start cranking and *then* slowly add handfuls of apples. If you're using an electric one, make sure it's running before you start throwing apples in.

6. **WHEN YOUR POMACE IS READY,** start filling the press. If it's a typical double-tub press, as rented at most home-brew stores, slide the pomace basket under the press and fold over the top of the cloth. Place the wood piece on top, and slowly start applying pressure. Crank it down a bit, then start another basket grinding.

7. **AFTER CRANKING THE PRESS DOWN** as far as you can, when you've gotten the last bit of juice out, unscrew the press, loosen up the pomace a bit, then try to repress it. You'll likely yield another cup or so, if you're lucky.

8. **WHEN YOUR JUICE BUCKET GETS FULL,** have another one ready to go, in order to catch any juice that comes out when you pull it away. And be sure to dump the fresh juice into your vessel.

9. **WHEN YOU'RE ALL DONE,** rinse the press down with a hose and make sure it's dry and clean before you store it or return it to the store.

Pressing the apples...
then making them alcoholic

1

Washing the apples.

2

This is a blend, so I will use Galas and Granny Smiths, shown here in the proportions I've decided on.

3

Inserting the screen into the grinder.

4

Mixing up One Step.

5

Putting One Step solution into fermentation vessel.

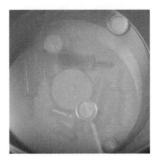

6

Cleaning airlocks in One Step solution.

7
Starting to drop clean apples into the grinder.

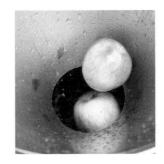

8
Apples in grinder.

9
It's faster to pour them out of a box than doing it one at a time; the grinder functions better then, as well.

10
Pomace left over in grinder after grinding.

11
Collecting the ground apples.

12
Checking the press to make sure it's ready.

13

Pouring apple pulp into the press.

14

Wrapping bag around pulp, ready for pressing.

15

The concentrated cider flowing into the container, ready for the yeast.

16

Pressing into bucket.

17

Using a "wine thief" to draw out some cider to test sugar levels.

18

Testing for sugar levels with a hydrometer.

19 Preparing the yeast.

20 Filling airlock with water.

21 Making note of the Specific Gravity that I measured with the hydrometer.

22 Leftover pomace.

CHAPTER
seven

RECIPES

BASIC DRY CIDER

INGREDIENTS
5 gallons juice
1 packet cider or champagne yeast
sulfites (if desired)

NOTES

Understanding how to make a basic, dry cider will lead to the ability to experiment later on. I see a lot of home cider makers come right out of the gate and attempt to make something pretty complex, without trying a simple dry cider first. Getting the basics down, and working out the initial kinks, is so important in making cider.

Also, in general I'd say people prefer a dry cider, so doing this right should be a crowd pleaser!

METHOD

With your base juice of choice, fill your vessel almost to the top. Make sure to take a measurement of your starting gravity, so you can determine the final alcohol and know when fermentation has stopped. Take your yeast, follow the specific instructions on the pack, and add the mix to the vessel. Seal the top with a clean and sanitized airlock. Add water to the airlock until the inside bit starts to float.

Optional: If you decide to put in sulfites, add the needed amount to the juice and let it sit for twenty-four hours before starting fermentation.

Fermentation time varies based on temperature, but in general you'll start to notice your airlock bubbling away in a few days. Fermentation usually takes seven to ten days, again depending on temperature and your starting gravity. During this time, you'll want to make sure the airlock and top are kept clean, and it may be necessary to remove the airlock and replace the water.

How do you know when fermentation is complete? Many rely on the "once the airlock stops moving" method, but the only way to truly know is to take a measurement with a hydrometer. Since this is a dry cider recipe, once it reads 1.000 or below, you're done with fermentation.

At this time it's wise to rack off into another clean vessel as soon as possible. Take your siphon – or pump, if you're lucky enough to have one – and rack above the lees (the very bottom of the vessel).

Put a new, sanitized airlock on the maturation vessel, and keep the batch as cool as possible for at least a month. At this point, when you decide to bottle or keg the cider is entirely up to you. Aging cider can do many different things, depending on your chosen blend. For example, harsh tannins will soften over time, and if left out long enough your cider could possibly have a malolactic fermentation, which adds a buttery/caramel note.

Resist the temptation to open the vessel often or taste the cider; you risk infection every time you open the vessel. Tasting once a month or so should be fine. Also, make sure to keep the vessel topped off with fermented cider, or water. You want to keep the maturation vessel as topped-off as possible, to lessen the risk of acetic bacteria forming and turning your hard work into a lot of vinegar.

Add sulfates to avoid malolactic fermentation

Malolactic fermentation (MLF, often shorthanded to ML) is the conversion of malic acid into lactic acid. Our winemaking counterparts use it quite a bit in making chardonnay, as it gives the wine its signature buttery, caramel-like flavor. As with anything else, you'll need to decide if you want to encourage this or prevent it.

Does MLF always occur? No

In what circumstances does MLF occur? When unsulfited cider is left on the lees. It's most common in high acid blends.

When is MLF good? When you want to round out the high acids, or to create a caramel-butterscotch taste.

When is MLF bad? If you have a low acid blend, or if you don't want the flavors associated with MLF (caramel, butterscotch).

How do you prevent MLF? You can avoid it by sulfating your cider after fermentation, and racking it off of its lees as quickly as you can after fermentation has stopped.

How do you encourage MLF? Most home brew stores that have a good selection of wine yeasts sell ML cultures that you can ad to your cider. To add, you'll want the temperature of your cider to be around 55 degrees or higher. Do not add it when you add the yeast, but instead when your specific gravity is around 1.01, so right before it goes completely dry.

My advice? Try to prevent MLF, especially when you first start. When you're more experienced go for it. You may like it, and it may become "your" style.

BUSHWHACKER SMOKED CIDER

I love anything smoked. We even have a house-smoked nut mix at the pubs, which we smoke over applewood, the same wood we use for this unique cider.

I started making this cider a few years ago. This is a recipe that requires you to press your own apples, so you may want to check with your local home-brew store to see if they rent apple grinders and presses.

The recipe also requires you to have a smoker of some sort. I use a Luhr Jensen Big Chief, with Luhr Jensen applewood chips. It would also work with other smokers and woods, as long as you have the ability to cold smoke.

The benefit of this cider is that you can use just about any apple, since the smoke will add so much flavor that "cider apples" aren't needed. Also, I don't smoke one-hundred percent of the apples for this; I just do about forty percent of the apples going into the batch.

Wash the apples before smoking, and allow them to completely dry. Set up your smoker for cold smoking, and smoke the apples for about two hours. Press them with the other apples, and ferment as normal.

The resulting cider will come out like a very peaty, smoky Scotch – think Islay or Highland Scotch. I would suggest at least a two-month maturation; this recipe also lends itself to dry oaking. Adding some crab apple juice can balance out the strong smoke flavor.

If you want the cider to taste less smoky, smoke fewer apples. I prefer this option to smoking them for less time.

NEW ENGLAND-STYLE CIDER

New England-style cider is characterized by the use of raisins, molasses, and brown or white sugar. It has, in general, a higher alcohol content; you'll be adding sugar before fermentation to boost the alcohol level. This is also a good recipe for playing around with oak chips, assuming you don't have space or access to an oak barrel. Here's my recipe for a New England-style cider:

4.5 gallons juice

1 lb brown sugar

8 oz dark Belgian candi sugar

1 Campden tablet, dissolved

6 oz dark roast oak chips

1 packet cider yeast

¾ pound raisins, dark

½ pound molasses

1 Fill a vessel with the juice of choice. Melt down the brown sugar and candi sugar in a pan. Allow the sugar to cool, then add it to the juice. Add your dissolved Campden tablet, and let the mix sit for twenty-four hours. At that time, record your specific gravity, and then add your yeast. You'll want to be at around 1.055 or higher for this batch, so if you're not there, add a bit more sugar.

2 Keep track of your SpGr, and once it reaches around 1.020, it's time to add your raisins and molasses. Boil the mix with a bit of cider for two minutes, then add the mix to your carboy. Let that sit until the gravity is at 1.000 or below. Rack off into a clean, sanitized vessel.

3 At this point, put your oak chips into a straining bag and simmer for ten minutes in some cider, then add the liquid to the vessel. If you have a vessel with a wide enough opening, go ahead and add the bag as well. If you do add the bag, don't let it sit for more than two weeks.

4 This is a batch that will age well, and one you'll want to let age. The high alcohol content will help protect against infection, but you'll still want to age it in as cool a place as you can.

5 For an added kick, try presoaking the oak chips for a few days in brandy, then infuse as directed above.

LINGONBERRY CIDER

Lingonberries are hard to find. I know, I've tried. They're associated with Scandinavia, and I hadn't run across a US cider company making a lingonberry cider. So I thought, what the hell, I'll do it.

This is a good time for absolute honesty. My secret to our lingonberry cider is using lingonberry *juice*, not berries. Simply put, I make a base of dry cider, and after the final rack, I add about twenty-four ounces of Lingonberry juice per five gallons. It adds a great color, and it has a very unique taste that catches people by surprise. At work, we call it "The Nihilist," a nod to one of my favorite movies, *The Big Lebowski.*

LOCAL CYSER

Cyser (or ceyser) is a cider that is blended with honey. If you want to get technical, it's less than fifty-percent honey. Any more, and you'd be making a mead with apple juice.

There are two ways to go about this. One, you could add the honey before you ferment. By doing so, you'll boost the juice's original gravity, making a nice high-alcohol finished product. The other option is to add it post-ferment, which will result in a stronger honey flavor, but won't add to the alcohol content. This is the version I prefer.

While any honey will work, it's way more fun to find a locally produced honey, and bring with it the nuances of the local flowers and plants. Plus, you'll end up with a cyser that can only be made in your area.

Searching farmers' markets is a great way to find local honey. Be warned, though: honey isn't cheap. It's often sold by the pound, and it can command a well-deserved high price. Ask your local supplier if they would be interested in a bulk discount; maybe you can even trade some of your final product for some honey. I've found cider to be an excellent trading tool!

When adding honey post-ferment, I suggest a pound per gallon. But how much you add depends on your taste.

When adding the honey, take a bit of your cider out and bring it to a simmer in a pan on your stove. Then slowly add the honey until it's completely dissolved. Let it cool, and add the mixture back to your vessel, keeping in mind how much room you have.

SCRUMPY

A very common question we get at the pubs is, "What's a scrumpy?" Well, let's start with what the word actually means. In Old English, to "scrump" fruit is to steal it – and more specifically, to steal apples. So, with scrumping there's not much choosing and planning going on; if you're scrumping, you're stealing whatever you can get your hands on. I should say here, please don't scrump apples.

So, a scrumpy these days refers to an assortment of apples – whatever could be obtained – made into a rough, unfiltered, usually higher-alcohol cider. Traditionally, a scrumpy was brewed by farmers who lacked the necessary equipment to create a more polished cider.

Another characteristic of a scrumpy is wild fermentation. Imagine a barn in the South West of England, full of wonderful wild yeast. There's a barrel in the corner. It may be fantastic, or it may be close to vinegar, but either way the scrumpy will be made with local fruit and will deliver a kick you won't soon forget.

So you want to make a scrumpy? Good for you! It's an excellent way to experiment with wild fermentation. Collect – legally! – a blend of local fruit. If at all possible, throw some crab apples in there. And don't be afraid to use a little bit of everything.

Make the cider as you normally would, but don't pitch any commercial yeast. And I wouldn't add sulfites, as they would likely (as is their purpose) kill off the native yeasts you're trying to foster.

Expect a slower ferment, and rack off only when fermentation has stopped, as measured by your hydrometer.

I wouldn't recommend any other additions, except perhaps for some oak chips. That way, you can get as close as possible to that great oaky, farmhouse taste without storing a fifty-five gallon barrel in your apartment.

CHERRY CIDER

Our cherry cider is one of the most popular flavored ciders in our pubs. We're lucky to have a lot of cherry orchards in the Pacific Northwest, and a lot of local producers put their own unique spin on this cider.

Black cherries or pie cherries are used most commonly. However, I've made cherry ciders with Rainier cherries, which are lighter and a little less intense, and I've had excellent results. In commercial cider making we typically add the cherries post-ferment, in the form of juice. Then – in larger scale production – we pasteurize the final product.

You can also make a fun twist on cherry cider by lightly mashing the cherries and fermenting them, as a sour beer producer might do. It will add a less intense cherry flavor, but it will also add some fermentable sugar to boost up your ABV.

I may be a bit biased, but "Oregon"-brand canned cherries are perfectly fine to use, and they're available at most grocery stores year-round. The reality is you may not have time to go cherry picking, or you may not be in an area with a lot of cherries growing nearby. This goes back to my philosophy: use what you have available, and don't stress about finding the perfect, ideal way of doing things.

Depending on your taste, you'll want to add at least four twelve-ounce cans of packed cherries. Or, if you use juice, I'd start with at least one half gallon per five-gallon vessel.

GINGER CIDER

Apple and ginger go hand in hand, so it's no surprise that almost every commercial cider maker makes a ginger cider. I don't personally like a lot of ginger ciders, but we make one at Bushwhacker because I know how much people like them!

The tricks with a ginger cider are regulating the balance of heat, and deciding on the method you'll use to infuse the cider. In my experience with spices, a light hand is more appreciated, overall, than a super spicy offering. But, if you and your friends like it hot, by all means go for it!

I've tried ginger fresh, powdered, and even crystalized. In my opinion, fresh ginger is the best. My favorite way to infuse is to juice the ginger – about eight ounces worth per five gallons, to start – and then go by taste after that.

If you don't have the ability to juice the fresh ginger, the other method I like is to make a "tea" using sliced ginger and some of the cider from the batch you're infusing.

My best advice when brewing a ginger cider is to slowly build it up, because it's a pain to try and get the ginger flavor dialed back once it's infused – which would require you to make it into a bigger batch and blend it out.

PEAR CIDER AND PERRY

Honestly, I could almost write a whole book on the virtues, techniques, and history of perry, or *poire* in France. Maybe if I'm lucky enough to make it to book number two, I'll tackle it.

The most important thing to understand for our purpose here is the difference between perry and pear cider. Simply put, perry is made with one-hundred percent pears, though some insist it can contain as much as twenty-five percent apples. Pear cider, on the other hand, is apple cider with pear juice added after fermentation to give it a robust, sweet, strong pear flavor.

Again, we find ourselves at the crossroads of tradition and innovation. Perry pears are used for "traditional, true" perry. They're a great fruit, small and tannic, and they provide an amazing final product. But . . . they're also hard to find and a pain to pick. And if you *are* lucky enough to locate them, they can be spendy.

You can certainly make a perry from pears available to you, such as D'Anjou, Bosc, or my favorite, Asian pears. These won't have the depth and complexity of a true perry pear, such as a Huffcap, Barland, Butt, or Thurston's Red, but I think you'll be quite pleased with the result.

Don't expect an overwhelming pear taste in your final product. A nice perry doesn't punch you in the face with pear flavor. It's subtle and can end up like a nice, light white wine.

What if you love pears, but don't feel like making a perry? Try making a pear cider. The most common way to do this is to add pear juice after you rack off of primary fermentation. To get that big bang of pear flavor you're no doubt expecting, add some pasteurized pear juice in at least a twenty-five-percent-pear-to-seventy-five-percent-apple ratio. As you rack off, reserve any extra cider you have left over to keep your vessel topped off.

Another trick of the trade, though I will say it's one I don't use, is to use pear flavoring, readily available at your local shop or online. The use of pear flavoring, or indeed any other "natural" flavoring, is a hotly debated topic among cider makers. If you look on the side of some of the more popular ciders, you may notice "flavoring" or "essence" being used. This is a bit of smoke-and-mirrors – a way to easily get the flavor you want without any risk of a secondary fermentation.

If you decide to go the route of using flavoring, you should use a very, *very* light hand; adding too much will ruin all of your hard work. Think two drops or less per five gallon batch, then let it sit, and taste. A little goes a very long way.

DRY OAKED CIDER

I've mentioned "dry oaking" cider. Oak chips are cheap and easy to get at any home-brew store, and they allow the home cider maker to impart an oak flavor without the hassles of using an actual barrel. That said, a lot of commercial cider makers use the dry oaking technique in order to avoid barrel use, and also to better control the oak flavor. Barrels are great, and fun to use, but they require a lot of knowledge to keep clean, and they also obviously require quite a bit of space.

Oak chips come in many different varieties, based on the type and char of the wood. The choice is entirely up to personal taste. I generally prefer a lighter toast; a strong oak flavor doesn't, in my opinion, lend itself well to cider.

Oak chips typically come in two- or eight-ounce bags, depending on the manufacturer. If your home-brew shop also services commercial makers, like mine does, larger bags are also available. How much you choose to use is entirely up to you, but at least four ounces for a five-gallon batch is recommended in order to achieve some flavor.

Jealous of those bourbon-barrel-aged ciders? Here's a little trick: soak your chips in your spirit of choice, then infuse the chips with your cider. And *boom*, you'll get the flavor you're going for without paying for a spent barrel from a distiller. The experimentation possibilities in doing this are endless. Going for a sake-barrel-aged flavor? Tequila? Soak the chips and infuse.

Here are the basics of infusing with oak chips: You'll want to create a tea with the chips. To make a "tea," put the oak chips in a mesh bag, and insert it into a pot with enough cider to cover the bag. Bring to a boil, then let simmer for about ten minutes. The darker the char, the less you'll want to steep it.

If you have a larger fermentation vessel, or something with a wider mouth, you can put the whole bag in. Just be careful not to over-oak it. If you go this route, you can still make a tea with it, but then you can also throw the whole bag into the cider for a more robust flavor.

SPANISH-STYLE CIDER

It's doubtful you will have access to the proper tools to make a true, Spanish cider. I'd guess you don't have a chestnut barrel lying around, or access to Basque varieties of apples, or some mind-blowing native Spanish yeast at your place. Even so, here are some tricks to help you get close.

First, sharp apples are a large part of a traditional Spanish-style blend. Assuming you don't have a Mokoa apple tree, you can try using varieties like Granny Smith, Foxwhelp, Brown's, Cap of Liberty, or a Rhode Island Greening. The next tip is to "infect" your cider with Brettanomyces. Brettanomyces is a family of yeasts used in the great farmhouse beers of Belgium and Germany. It's what you add, either by hand or naturally, to get that classic farmhouse flavor. You can buy Brett – as it's commonly called – in a package at most home-brew stores. This will help give it the classic funk of most Basque or Asturian ciders, without storing your cider in a barn or shed that has developed wild yeasts over several hundred years. Cheating a bit? Yeah, but I promise it'll be fun. You'll want to add the Brett pack at primary fermentation, and make sure to keep your batch a bit warmer than normal – around sixty-eight to seventy degrees.

This is also a batch you won't want to carbonate or age for too long. Also, once you're confident enough to do so, this would be a great batch to let the native yeasts go nuts in. If you decide to pitch a yeast, choose something like cider yeast in order to avoid infusing any other nuances besides the Brett.

Often, I get home-brew batches that went off, and the maker exclaims, "It's just a farmhouse style cider." But it's not. It's infected . . . in a bad way. Understanding faults – and understanding funk – takes time and patience.

Another note when dealing with Brett: make sure to thoroughly clean any and all equipment during this process. Brett can easily infect your whole setup if you don't take the proper precautions – giving everything you make a bit of a Brett flavor.

CRANBERRY CIDER

Nothing screams "holidays" like a well-crated cranberry cider. Commercially speaking, it's not a super common flavor – curiously – but I do try to make one at the pub every year. As with other recipes, you can certainly add cranberry juice post-ferment, but this is one example where I would highly recommend buying fresh or frozen cranberries if at all possible, and juicing those. Normally what I do is juice the cranberries, then put any of the leftover solids in a straining bag, and put that into the vessel.

If you use cranberry juice, try to find the most pure juice you can, and try to stay away from a cranberry juice "cocktail."

A fun element to blend with this is a bit of ginger root. Adding spices like cinnamon and cloves is also common. If you go that route, be careful to use a light hand, as a little bit of either goes a long way. For example, if I make a spiced cider, I don't use more than one cinnamon stick per five gallons.

HIGH-GRAVITY CIDER

So, you have a goal: to make something on the higher alcohol side of things. Without adding sugar of any kind, your cider will probably end up at between five and six-and-a-half percent on its own, which is just fine for most people. Most commercial producers stay below seven percent to avoid paying a higher tax rate per gallon. But at home, if you so desire, why not go nuts?!

It's time to learn a new word: chaptalization.

When you chaptalize something, you're simply adding more fermentable sugar before you add the yeast, and therefore raising the specific gravity of your juice. You'll also need to make sure the yeast you choose can handle fermenting a higher alcohol product. For example, Wyeast Cider Yeast has an alcohol tolerance of up to twelve percent, so if you go nuts and go for something higher, you'll want to choose a yeast strain that can handle it.

Besides making a boozier booze, another reason to chaptalize is to raise the alcohol of a low-gravity juice, in order to prevent infection. If you start with anything south of 1.045, it's best to add sugar of some sort to get up to at least that level.

Two ounces of sugar per gallon will raise the specific gravity about .005, give or take. Depending on your choice of sugar – be it white, brown, turbinado, etc. – the results may differ. Honey is also a great way to add some sugar, but to achieve the same results you'll want about three ounces per gallon instead of two.

BUSHWHACKER ITALIAN PLUM CIDER

A year or so ago at the pub we received a treat: some donated Italian Plums. I decided to do what felt right with them, make alcohol!

For this recipe I did something a bit different: I fermented the plums. For a five gallon batch, I used about eight pounds of plums. I also added twelve ounces of dark Belgian candi sugar pre-ferment. I did the initial ferment in a thirty-liter plastic fermentation vessel, using a blend of locally sourced Akane apples. After primary, I racked off into a five-gallon wood barrel, keeping about a gallon aside to top off the barrel from time to time. After aging it for about three months, I racked again into a keg, force carbed for forty-eight hours, then threw it on tap – to much approval.

Experimenting with fermenting on the added fruit is something I'd like to do more, and would encourage you to do. Make sure you get the pieces small enough to be able to easily get them out after you rack and clean out your primary fermentation vessel.

You likely won't see a noticeable effect on your OG (original specific gravity) since the fruit hasn't broken down yet, but it will indeed add extra booze.

I think most stone fruit would lend itself nicely to this technique, and experimenting with plums, peaches, apricots, or others would yield interesting results. If you add the juice after ferment – right before bottling or kegging – expect a relatively subtle flavor instead of something more intense.

SPICED CIDER

For some, nothing beats a great mulled cider during the cold winter months. At our pubs, we have a crock-pot full of some nice warm cider to help warm our customers as they come in. There are two ways to do this.

Start with a semi-dry to semi-sweet base cider. For a gallon, infuse one cinnamon stick, three cloves, some dried ginger, and a bit of nutmeg to taste. The most important thing is to not let the cinnamon or cloves sit for too long, or the taste will become quite bitter. At the pub, we put the cloves in a tea strainer, so they're easy to pull out once the flavor has been added.

If you want to make a mulled cider batch from scratch, the key is to tart with a light hand, and build it up. Start with your basic dry cider recipe, then add the spices about two weeks after you rack off to mature.

I would advise not adding a whole cinnamon stick or cloves to your batch. Instead, make a tea from your existing juice. Then, after allowing it to cool down, add the juice back to the cider. If you simply put in the cloves or cinnamon, the results could be disastrous; the cider might become quite bitter or be stronger than you would have liked.

SWEET CIDER

Making a good, sweet cider is a bit tricky. You'd think you could just add a bunch of sugar to achieve this, but by now I hope you know that sugar adds to the alcohol content, but not to the sweetness. The trick to making your cider sweeter is to do a juice add-back, or a sugar add-back, after fermentation has stopped. The risk here is, if there's any yeast left you'll have your cider go into a secondary fermentation, and possibly create a bottle bomb in the process.

But here's how to do it without this danger.

Start with your basic dry recipe, and finish it to your liking. Now, here comes the dirty little secret. The best way to add sweetness is to add fresh juice back, which is easy on a commercial scale with all the sterile filtration and pasteurizing equipment available to kill any and all yeast cells left. It's doubtful you have any of this equipment. So, here are two safe ways I recommend:

Add a non-reactive sugar like Xylitol or Stevia to your batch. It will sweeten it up, but any leftover yeast will not eat it. This is not even close to "traditional," but it will work.

Add fresh juice back, bottle the cider, and then pasteurize in the bottle. Note: wear proper safety glasses and gloves, and use common sense during this process.

To in-bottle pasteurize, you'll take your filled, back-sweetened bottles and submerge them in a pot of water on your stovetop. Slowly bring the water temperature to 180 degrees, which will make the inside cider temperature about 165 degrees. Hold this temperature for ten minutes, then bring the temperature back down. At this point, your cider should be pasteurized, and the risk for any bottle bombs, even with the juice added, should be minimal.

Mastering these techniques will add to your creative potential, and will also allow you to explore a wide array of different flavors. There's a lot of debate over pasteurized versus non-pasteurized ciders. And there is indeed a taste difference, if you try the same batches side by side. But if you make a large batch, and you want to back-sweeten, pasteurization is really the best way to go to avoid any issues.

BUSHWHACKER ALICE

Named after my grandmother, Alice has quickly become one of our most popular ciders, both at the pub and out in the market. Not one for keeping secrets, I'm proud to share my recipe for it.

The backbone of this cider is the use of *only* Granny Smith apples. I wanted to figure out a good way to use these apples, since they grow in abundance in the Northwest and are available year round, either from stores or from the cold storage of larger orchardists.

This is also a good example of practicing what I preach: in a pinch, I use my good relationship with our local produce stand to purchase one bin at a time of Granny Smiths at a great discount!

For the recipe, I blend two different yeasts together, both made by Wyeast Laboratories in Hood River, Oregon. I use a fifty-fifty blend of their Cider yeast and their French Saison.

The other aspect of this cider is its clarity: Alice is crystal clear, well-carbonated, and crisp. To achieve this at my cidery, I cold crash it for at least a week, then rack off the top. At home, if you can't cold crash and you want it clear, giving yourself extra time – or using the aforementioned caring agents will also work.

Note: "Cold crashing" is a technique that involves lowering the temperature of the cider, to just above freezing if possible, in order to force the spent yeast to the bottom of the vessel. Then, you "rack off the top," meaning you rack off, being careful not to put the racking cane all the way to the bottom; otherwise you'll just suck up everything you forced down, making the process ineffective. This is a way to naturally clear up a cider.

FORGOTTEN TRAIL

Our very first flagship cider, Forgotten Trail, was named after an inside joke between my wife and I. It refers to the time and energy it takes to run a business, and how entrepreneurs unfortunately don't get to enjoy some activities the way they once did. So, Forgotten Trail: a trail that you may have forgotten about with the stress and speed of a busy life.

Forgotten Trail is a semi-dry cider, unfiltered, with a mix of dessert fruit. I use this ratio:

15% Red Delicious • 45% Braeburn • 15% Golden Delicious • 25% Jonagold

The apples are all ground and pressed together. For this batch, I only use one yeast: Wyeast Cider yeast. I add no sugar or sulfites before fermentation.

I usually start with a SpGr of around 1.053, which results in a cider of 6.9% ABV. At sixty-five degrees, the batch usually finishes off at 1.00 SpGr in about eight days. I rack it off, then top it off with some Forgotten Trail I have from another batch, to make sure to keep the tank full. Water can be used in place of more cider, but it should only be a cup or less.

Since the mix of apples consists entirely of dessert fruit, the required maturation time is relatively short. I let it sit for thirty days, then taste.

I like to put this cider right into the kegs at this point, so it can stay cold and in order to avoid the necessity of sterile filters, pasteurization, or sulfites. I usually make this in five-hundred liter batches at our Brooklyn pub.

The resulting cider is semi-dry, with a slight haze to it.

HOW TO
TASTE
CIDER

*Each person's palette is different.
We all bring a lot of conscious
and subconscious thoughts to the
table when we taste a cider.*

I ALWAYS SUGGEST to those who are tasting commercial ciders and want to learn to be somewhat critical: do it blind.

At Bushwhacker, we regularly set up tastings with some of our suppliers. But subconsciously, labeling, packaging, and whatever feelings you have about a particular company can affect how you taste the final product.

Likewise, when a company hosts a tasting, I'm sure some of the company representatives "click" better with certain customers than with others, and I can't help but think that has some effect on the tasting experience. Still, tastings are a great way to allow customers to come in and taste through a singular brand's lineup for no charge.

I would suggest that you take an assortment of bottles home and have some fun setting up your own tasting. In this chapter I want to go over how to set up your own tasting at home, and also how to look for characteristics and faults that will ultimately make you a stronger cider maker.

Tasting at home:

1. DON'T BRING TOO MANY CIDERS. I think five or six is about as many as you would want to critically taste in any given setting. Any more than that and your palette will get confused.

I've judged a few events, and gone through a marathon of up to thirty tastes! I can honestly tell you that after ten or so, I was quite useless. It has nothing to do with intoxication; I just became less and less able to be critical and observant.

There are, of course, people trained to do long stretches of tastings, but I'm certainly not one of them. I'd say ten to fifteen in a row is my personal limit. Start out with five or six if you're tasting to learn. But go nuts if you just want to have some fun and enjoy some great cider . . . and, of course, if you aren't driving home!

2. HAVE SOME FOOD. I'm very open about the fact that I may be one of the worst people to suggest food pairings with cider. Take cheese, for example. I love cheese, and I love cider, so in my little mind all cheese and cider go together!

Cheese is the classic go-to with cider, but it's obviously not the be-all and end-all. Raw walnuts, crackers, charcuterie, or some breads also go well when you're tasting. Make sure to pick light-flavored food so as not to overpower your taste buds or affect the flavor of the cider. For example, I don't think a burrito with extra jalapenos would be the best food choice while critically tasting cider. I'm not saying a burrito and cider don't make for a good afternoon, but the burrito will assuredly ruin your tasting skills. Another fun thing: if you go the cheese route, try to pick some cheeses that are from the same geographic area as your selected ciders.

3. GLASSWARE. In case you haven't noticed, there's a ton of glassware, in all shapes and sizes, on the market. There is some science behind the shapes, allowing certain flavors to be enhanced.

I'm a little conservative when it comes to glassware. I understand the reasoning behind it, but I also don't think we all need a thousand different glassware styles in our homes. I like cider in a simple pint glass, and I also use pint glasses if I'm doing a tasting for friends. At work, though, I prefer a smaller size, something like a small white wine glass with a stem, so I don't warm up the glass too much with my hands. Whatever you choose, make sure you get a clear glass so you can take note of the coloring of the cider.

4. CALM DOWN ON THE SWIRL. One of the most obvious pieces of advice I got long ago was to not go nuts on the swirl. It's the classic move to grab a wine or cider and – before it even gets to your nose – to create a minor whirlpool in the glass.

Swirling certainly opens up the beverage and allows your nose to pick out more of the subtle aromas, but here's the trick: do a pre-sniff. To really see how the swirl changes it, smell it first, and *then* open it up with a *gentle* swirl. Swirling first is sort of like adding salt or pepper to a dish before you even try it.

5. H2O IS YOUR FRIEND. In addition to having a bit of water to cleanse your palette between tastes, it's also handy to have some nearby to rinse your glass out. Some flavors will cling to the glass, and you'll want to rinse between – unless, of course, you have a plethora of glassware at your disposal and enjoy doing dishes.

6. TAKE NOTES. If you're looking to learn, it's very important to take notes – ideally, ones you can read later. This is a great example of "do as I say, not as I do." I'm horrible at taking notes, but I'm working on being better. I've tasted a ton of ciders in the years since we opened Bushwhacker, and I regret not having notes on all of them.

There are little score sheets you can set up on your own or find online, but even just a note or two can trigger memories and allow you to recall a particular cider. When I do take notes, I also employ a ten-point system, indicating whether I liked the cider or not.

Having notes is also super helpful when you're talking to your local cider maker – which I hope is Bushwhacker if you're in Portland! We handle a lot of different ciders, and we always try to help, but once in a while I see a customer come in looking for "a cider I had a few months ago . . . that was sweet . . . that I loved . . ." Obviously, that's not a lot for us to go on.

I have a few customers who bring out a little notebook and ask me for something specific. That allows us to bend over backwards trying to find it, order it, or find out when it's coming back.

So, let's set up a tasting!

There are several ways to go about this, and these are only suggestions:

Geography:
At Bushwhacker, we arrange our coolers geographically, then alphabetically. A tasting featuring ciders based in a particular state or country can be a lot of fun. Country tastings can be a great way to learn about styles as well. A US tasting, obviously, would yield a lot of different styles.

Cans:

Of the top-ten bestselling ciders at our southeast Portland pub, eight are canned ciders. We've seen, and continue to see, a huge growth in the canned cider market. And why not? Cans are great for golfing, beaches, marinas, camping, and anywhere else glass is not a good option or isn't allowed.

The other cool thing is, cans are now being filled with really good cider, smashing the preconceived notion that cans are only for cheap, mass-produced ciders. Sitting down and tasting a lineup of canned ciders would be a lot of fun. Scratch that – it *is* a lot of fun!

Styles & Recipes:

An obvious choice is to line up ciders by style. How about a lineup of all cherry ciders? All dry ciders? All hop ciders? This is a quick way to figure out your favorites, and also to find a recipe you might want to clone or add your own twist to. However, since you'll be tasting a bunch of relatively similar ciders, make sure you follow my suggestion of drinking water in between, rinsing your glasses, and having some food to help cleanse your palette between.

For example, we carry several different cherry ciders at our pubs, but they all taste different. If you tried them all next to one another with nothing in between, I suspect the subtle flavor differences would be lost on anything less than an extremely well-seasoned palette.

Vintages:

Not many ciders are vintage-dated, due to rules laid out by the US government concerning cider. That being said, if you have a nice cellar at home and have the resolve to not guzzle it all, you can keep your own selection of vintage ciders. Also, pay attention to labels and you'll find that often ciders have batch dates, with a clear year code printed on them.

Now's a good time to talk about cellaring ciders:

I often get asked at Bushwhacker about cellaring ciders. This is a great way to see how a cider ages, and also to keep on-hand a cider you love that isn't available year around. Here are some things to keep in mind:

1. **AGING A BORING CIDER** won't turn it into a great cider. Here's an example from the beer world: do you think putting that sixteen-ounce can of Pabst Blue Ribbon down for a few years will turn it into something extraordinary? Think again. Putting a less-than-exciting cider down to age won't "improve" it. It will likely taste exactly the same, even after several months or years.

2. **AS WITH BEER,** the higher the ABV, the better suited a cider is to aging. Think of ciders with seven percent ABV or greater. The higher alcohol content will prevent against infection.

3. **THE IDEAL CELLARING DURATION** for most ciders is two years. Though, with all the new cider makers that have come up, we're still seeing how certain ciders age. Also, be aware that most smaller producers don't pasteurize, so at a certain point instead of having a great bottle of cider you'll just end up with a great bottle of vinegar. The perfect situation would be to have several bottles of the same cider, and pull one every six months or so.

4. **UNDERSTAND CELLAR TEMPS.** The classic temperature zone for a cellar is fifty to fifty-five degrees. Same goes for cider. Have a fridge you're keeping it all in? That's fine. Just don't expect the cider to develop as much at a cooler temperature.

5. **IF YOU WANT TO AGE YOUR OWN** homemade ciders, consider wax-sealing the bottles. Besides regulating temperature, keeping oxygen from getting into your bottle is critical. If you don't want to wax your bottles, consider spending a bit more and investing in oxygen-absorbing bottle caps, which are available at most home-brew stores.

Terms:

Having a basic understanding of terms associated with cider will make you a better taster – and it will also make you sound fancy when you talk to your friends!

ACETIC: A commercial producer fears nothing more than acetic bacteria, which creates vinegar. A touch of acetic can be appreciated, as it is in most Spanish ciders, but too much acetic can turn that labored-over cider into salad dressing. The best defense against developing acetic bacteria in your own cider is to eliminate as much oxygen in your batch as possible; this means, once you rack off from primary, keep your vessel filled to the brim!

Outside of a Spanish-style cider, if you tasted acetic in a commercial cider, it would generally be considered a major fault.

MOUTH: This is how the cider feels on your palette, or to be more literal, in your mouth. Consider the body of it. Is it light? Heavy?

NOSE: The cider's aroma. As I said, take note of what you pick up before you swirl it around, and then again after. Do you get a hint of vanilla or tobacco from a barrel-aged cider? A bit of sulfur, perhaps, from a cider that was oversulfated (think of the smell when you light a match, or the smell of eggs). Did the nose lead to a taste you expected? Or did it lead you astray?

FINISH: The lasting impression. Did it finish dry? Sweet? A good, strong tannic cider will almost leave you thirsty!

ACIDIC: Knowing how to describe acidity is a good skill. The main acid to look out for is malic acid. Malic acid exists in all apples, in various levels. We'll often balance the levels out in a low-acid juice, using store-bought malic acid. Of course, you can do this as well. Once you've experienced tasting too much malic acid, you can easily spot it. Want a good example? For an apple that's very high in acid, think Granny Smith; Golden Delicious is a good example of a low-acid apple.

TANNINS: The classic way to describe tannins is, "Think of raw walnuts." It's the effect of drying out your mouth. You can also see the chemical effects of tannins by cutting open an apple: in general, the faster the apple turns brown, the higher the fruit's tannin level. If you're a wine person, think of the difference between a red wine and white wine. The red will have more tannins.

STILL VS. FLAT: As I've mentioned elsewhere in the book, still is a *choice* and flat is a *fault*. Still ciders are tough for most consumers to enjoy. Most people expect a bit of a fizz in their finished cider. How we get there differs from style. Do we force carb? Perform a *méthode champenoise* – the traditional method of carbonating champagne? Or do we use priming sugar as we bottle?

Take note on a sparkling cider of the size of the bubbles. Force-carbonation, which the majority of commercial cider producers – including myself – perform, results in big bubbles, while a natural carbonation has finer, champagne-like bubbles.

Lack of carbonation is only a fault if it goes against what the producer, or home maker, was trying to achieve.

CLARITY: This is how the cider looks. Is it hazy? Crystal clear? Usually the appearance is a choice, either by design or due to access to certain equipment. Our Granny Smith cider, Alice, is purposefully filtered to make it almost completely clear, because in my head that's how I saw a Granny Smith cider appearing. By contrast, we purposefully don't make our Forgotten Trail cider quite as clear; I wanted it to have a slight haze.

CHAPTER
nine

COOKING
WITH
CIDER

---

*Here is a collection of recipes,
developed by our talented culinary
team at Bushwhacker Woodlawn.*

BUSHWHACKER CIDER VINAIGRETTE

4 shallots

1 cup cider. At our pub,
we use our own Granny Smith
cider, Alice.

2 tablespoons honey

8 tablespoons vinegar

4 tablespoons Dijon mustard

2 cups oil

Roast the shallots, then combine the shallots, cider, honey, vinegar, and Dijon mustard into a food processor. Combine ingredients until smooth. Slowly drizzle the oil in, allowing everything to continue to combine after all the oil is added. Taste, and season with salt and pepper.

APPLE COLESLAW

---

1 head of cabbage

3 peeled carrots

3 apples

1 cup pickled red onion

2 tablespoons fennel seeds

2 tablespoons coriander

1 cup mayo

¼ cup apple cider vinegar

1 bunch picked cilantro

Salt

Pepper

Julienne the cabbage, carrots, and apples, and toss them together. Toast your fennel seeds and coriander together in a sauté pan over medium-high heat for two minutes. Put this mixture into a spice grinder and grind into a fine powder. Toss the powder in with the vegetable mixture.

Add the remaining ingredients, and season with salt and pepper to taste. Mix it all together, and eureka! Your slaw is done. If you like it creamier, add more mayo. For less creamy, reduce the mayo.

Enjoy!

PULLED PORK BUTT

(requires smoker)

---

1 five-pound pork butt

2 cups salt

Trim seventy percent of the fat off the pork butt. Take a paper towel and dry off the butt, then coat the butt in salt and let it sit uncovered in the fridge for twelve to twenty-four hours.

When you're ready to smoke the pork, take it out of the fridge and pat it dry. After the pork is dry, make your rub (recipe follows) and thoroughly coat the meat.

Pork rub

¾ cup brown sugar

¾ cup white sugar

½ cup paprika

¼ cup garlic powder

2 tablespoons pepper

2 tablespoons ginger powder

2 tablespoons onion powder

Once your meat is thoroughly coated in the rub, throw the butt in the smoker for at least three hours, along with your favorite choice of wood chips. Obviously, we only use apple wood!

While the pork is smoking, start putting together your braising liquid.

Braising liquid

5 carrots, roughly chopped

5 celery stalks, roughly chopped

3 yellow onions, roughly chopped

7 Roma tomatoes

¼ cup red wine vinegar

¼ cup brown sugar

1 bunch thyme

8 garlic cloves

2 tablespoons mustard seeds

2 tablespoons Worcestershire sauce

7 quarts cider. At the pub, we use our very own Forgotten Trail cider, which is a semi-dry cider.

Combine the carrots, celery, and onions into a pan large enough to hold your pork butt plus some extra liquid. Add the Roma tomatoes, garlic, thyme, and mustard seeds.

Sweat the vegetables down until tender. Once they're tender, add all the other ingredients and bring everything to a boil.

When your pork is done smoking, add it to your braising liquid, making sure the liquid covers all of the butt. Put a lid on the pot, and place in an oven at three-hundred degrees for three hours or so. You'll know it's done when it either falls apart or reaches an internal temperature of 195. If it's not pulling apart at 195, put it into the oven until the butt reaches 203 degrees.

At the pub, we serve it on a brioche bun, with a bit of apple coleslaw on the side!

CIDER HOUSE FONDUE

At the pub, we serve this alongside rustic bread, roasted carrots, cauliflower, apple slices, and sausage.

---

1 small, diced shallot

3 tablespoons apple cider vinegar

3 pounds Gruyère cheese, grated

4 tablespoons corn starch

3 cups cider. In the pub, we use locally produced farmhouse cider. Any dry cider would work just fine.

¼ cup apple Brandy or Calvados

Bring the cider and vinegar to a simmer, and reduce to low heat.

Toss the grated cheese with cornstarch.

Slowly add the cheese, a handful at a time, stirring after each addition.

Continue to add a little cheese at a time, stirring as you go.

Once all the cheese is added, increase the heat to medium until the fondue bubbles.

Stir constantly, and then add the brandy. Season with pepper, and keep warm to serve.

CHAPTER
ten

CIDER
COCKTAILS

As I write this book, we just got our full liquor license at our Woodlawn pub. Besides carrying apple Brandy and Calvados, we've also come up with a great selection of cider-focused cocktails.

IT WAS IMPORTANT FOR ME to encourage innovation, and not to simply provide cocktails that added one spirit to a cider and called it a cocktail! Following are some recipes developed by our dynamic bar manager, KC Yenne.

POMMEAU MANHATTAN

1¼ oz. Bulleit Rye

¾ oz. EZ Orchards Pommeau

2 dashes Angostura bitters

Add all ingredients, add ice, and stir, served up.

While we decided to use the EZ Orchards Pommeau, any high-quality Pommeau would be acceptable.

BUSHWHACKER G&T

1¼ oz. Aria gin

5 oz. tonic

3 slices apple

1 slice of lime

Muddle the apple and lime, then add gin and ice. Shake and serve in a rocks glass, topped with tonic.

APPLE BRANDY "CIDE-CAR"

––––––––––

1¼ oz. Lairds Apple Brandy

2 slices orange

1 slice lemon

½ oz. honey

Muddle the orange and lemon together, then add the honey and brandy, add ice, shake, and serve up in snifter.

CHERRY 88

––––––––––

1¼ oz. Portland 88 vodka

8 oz. Blue Mt. Cherry Cider

1 oz. lemon-lime soda

Add ice to Portland 88 vodka, fill halfway with Blue Mt. Cherry Cider, and top with lemon-lime soda.

Note: We have a great friendship with the folks at Blue Mountain, and we've carried their Cherry Cider since the day we first opened our Brooklyn (Portland) pub in 2001. This is a great cherry cider on its own, but it always screamed to be made into a cocktail. You can certainly use another cherry cider, but if you can get the Blue Mountain, it really is perfect!

CIDER MULE

1¼ oz. Portland 88 vodka

lime

2 dashes Angostura bitters

6 oz. Bushwhacker Alice Cider

2-3 oz. lemon-lime soda

Muddle lime, add Portland 88 and two dashes of Angostura, then top with Alice and lemon-lime soda. Serve in a copper mug, if you have one.

Note: Alice is our own single-varietal Granny Smith cider. If you're outside the Portland area, try using another tart, light cider in the Alice's place.

FORGETFUL ROB

---

1 oz. Laphroaig Single Malt

3 oz. Forgotten Trail cider

2 dashes Angostura bitters

Combine ingredients, add ice, and stir. Serve in a rocks glass, on the rocks.

Note: Forgotten Trail is a semi-dry, clean cider that we make. Any good session cider will work as well.

BASQUE-TINI

1¼ oz. Portland 88 vodka

½ oz. Sarasola Basque cider

½ oz. olive juice

Combine ingredients, add ice, and stir. Served up.

Note: I challenged our staff to come up with a cocktail using a Spanish cider. We chose the Sarasola Basque cider to start, but any still cider from the Asturias or Basque regions would work equally well. If you're a fan of a good dirty martini, this drink is for you!

CIDER DARK & STORMY

1½ oz. Gosling's Dark Rum

5 oz. Thistly Cross Ginger Cider

splash ginger ale

Combine ingredients, and serve with a lime garnish.

CIDER JULEP

sugar cube

2-3 sprigs fresh mint

1½ oz. rye whisky of choice
(at the pub we use Bulleit Rye)

5 oz. Seattle Cider Co. Basil Mint Cider

Muddle sugar and mint. Mix in whiskey and top off with mint cider.

APPLE COSMO

¾ oz. vodka of choice

3 oz. Bushwhacker Alice Cider

3 oz. cranberry Juice

Stir ingredients together and strain, Serve up with apple-slice garnish.

BIG APPLE ICED TEA

½ oz. vodka

½ oz. gin

½ oz. rum

3-4 oz. lemon cider

splash cola

Shake ingredients together, then top with lemon cider and cola.

Note: If you can't find a lemon cider in your area, use a regular dry cider, and add one ounce of fresh lemon juice.

CHAPTER
eleven

RESOURCES

A lot of good people out there are passionate about cider.

Blogs:

I should note, I don't necessarily agree with what these writers put out. In fact, often I don't. But these people are passionate, and I respect that immensely. I've met most of them, and they are damn nice people. I recommend these blogs because they're well-written, and I get a lot of enjoyment and education by reading them.

IAMCIDER
billbradshaw.co.uk/cider

Serious Eats
drinks.seriouseats.com/cider/

Cider Monger
cidermonger.com/

The Cider Digest
www.talisman.com/cider

Old Time Cider
www.oldtimecider.com/

Old Scrump's Cider House
www.ciderandperry.co.uk/

Organizations:

Here are a few of organizations across the country that support cider. Take them for what they're worth; they normally require a fee to be a member, so they promote their own members exclusively. Again, they're passionate and they care about the industry, but they are not one-hundred percent unbiased.

Northwest Cider Association:
www.nwcider.com/

Great Lakes International Cider & Perry Association
hosts of the popular GLINTCAP award ceremony.
www.greatlakescider.com/

Rocky Mountain Cider Association
www.rmcider.org/Home.html

Vermont Ice Cider Association
www.vermonticecider.com/

United States Cider Association
www.ciderassociation.org/

CAMRA (Campaign for Real Ale)
www.camra.org.uk/
about-cider-perry

Events:

Cider festivals of any kind or size feel very different than a wine or beer fest. I'm not even sure it's possible to put into words why, but I'll try.

The masses understand beer and wine for the most part, but cider is still a new thing for a lot of people, and I sense a clear, wonderful open-mindedness at cider fests. There doesn't seem to be that "we've seen it all already" mentality that you see at beer festivals, and the producers are still excited to be there. The list of festivals is growing, and I'll list the ones I know to be going strong at the time of writing.

Cider Summit

Portland, OR; Seattle, WA; San Francisco, CA; Chicago, IL

Alan Shapiro, founder of the Cider Summit series, has arguably done more for cider in the United States than any actual cider maker. Cider Summit, started in Seattle, has expanded to two-day events across the country, attracting thousands of cider lovers. No beer, wine, or mead is allowed at these events, yet the line to get in is staggering. We're proud to be a supporting sponsor of the Portland Cider Summit, now in its fifth year.

August in Port Townsend, WA

Held in picturesque Port Townsend, Summer Cider Days is a great ongoing event focusing on cider made in the Pacific Northwest.

Cider Weeks

Oregon, Washington, Finger Lakes, Vermont, Virginia, and more starting all the time!

Cider weeks are held all over the country, sometimes tagged onto an existing event, like Cider Summit. Usually, they involve various events throughout a certain area, held at different bars, bottle shops, and producers.

Franklin County Cider Days

November in Massachusetts

A festival I haven't had the privilege of attending, this is held in Massachusetts in November, and involves all the things that makes a festival great! There are tastings, talks, and even a competition.

Great Lakes Cider and Perry Festival

summer in the Midwest

This very well-known and popular festival is home to the prestigious GLINTCAP award, held in high regard as an advertising tool with cider makers.

Country-specific cider terms:

Basque region of Spain

- **ardo:** wine
- **barrikotea:** wood barrel, up to one-hundred liters

- **dolare:** press

- **kizkia:** a tool used to collect apples

- **patsa:** pomace

- **sagar:** apple

- **sagardoa:** Basque term for cider

- **sagardotegi:** Basque cider house

- **sagasti:** apple orchard

- **sidra:** Asturian term for cider

- **upelategi:** barrel house

France

- **brut:** Indicates a dry cider

- **chapeau brun:** the brown cap resulting from a successful keeving

- **cidre:** French term for cider

- **cidre Bouche:** a sparkling cider bottled with a cork and cage

- **doux:** indicates a sweet cider

- **Pays d'Auge:** region of Normandy

- **poire:** perry

- **pomme:** apple

England

- **Cyder:** alternate spelling of cider

- **Draught:** a draft cider

- **Panking pole:** a long pole, usually with a hook, used to get apples off the tree.

- **Scrump:** to steal fruit, mainly apples. Also refers to a traditional, still, cloudy cider.

- **Tallet:** a loft in a barn used to store apples before pressing.

- **Tump:** a hill, or mound of apples.

Germany

- **Apfelwien:** German term for cider

- **Bembei:** Apfelwien jug

- **Geripptes:** traditional cider glass, with cuts in it to give it a good grip

- **halbtrocken:** indicates a semi-dry cider

- **Hesse:** the most popular region for cider production and consumption

- **saurer Most:** sour must

- **trocken:** indicates a dry cider

Cider-making terms:

ABV: alcohol by volume

ABW: alcohol by weight

acetic acid: bacteria that forms in presence of oxygen, turns into vinegar

Brettanomyces (Brett): a yeast that creates the "farmhouse" style funk

dry cider: cider that has very little, or no sweetness

Brix: sugar content of liquid.

ciderkin: a very low alcohol cider made from adding water to dry pomace.

farmhouse cider: rough, rustic cider, usually with strong hints of Brett.

hoop: the round metal piece that goes around a barrel

keeving: a complex process, most notably used by French producers resulting in a naturally sweet, low-alcohol cider.

lees: the insoluble matter that is at the bottom of a fermentation, or maturation vessel.

malic acid: the main acid found in apples

milling: to grind the apples

OG: original gravity

Pasteurization: heating up the cider, either in the bottle or in bulk, to kill any bacteria or yeast and to help it be shelf stable.

pitching (yeast): to add yeast to your juice

pomace: the result of grinding apples

racking: to pump, or siphon, liquid from one vessel to another

stave: the wood pieces that make up a barrel

TG: Terminal Gravity, the gravity level after fermentation has stopped.

photo credits

Unless otherwise indicated, all photography courtesy of the author.

Page i, ii: © rez-art/iStockphoto.com; xi: © pjohnson1/iStockphoto.com; xii: © bhofack2/iStockphoto.com; 1, 7, 19, 41, 59, 69, 83, 109, 119, 127, 137: © Hanis/iStockphoto.com; 6, 102: © Veronika Roosimaa/iStockphoto.com; 18: © Pgiam/iStockphoto.com; 25: © Andrew Cribb/iStockphoto.com; 27, 33: © Murphy_Shewchuk/iStockphoto.com; 28: © slobo/iStockphoto.com; 29: © fotokostic/iStockphoto.com; 30: © sykadelx/iStockphoto.com; 31: © Anna_Rostova; 32: © GomezDavid/iStockphoto.com; 34: © Julie Marshall/iStockphoto.com; 35: © kcline/iStockphoto.com; 36: © Roel Smart/iStockphoto.com; 37: © Nancy Tunison/iStockphoto.com; 38: © JVisentin/iStockphoto.com; 39: © trinetuzun/iStockphoto.com; 40: © matejphoto/iStockphoto.com; 48: © PaulCowan/iStockphoto.com; 52: © ChiccoDodiFC/iStockphoto.com; 68: © Carsthets/iStockphoto.com; 74: © Bignai/iStockphoto.com; 82, 131: © Lauri Patterson/iStockphoto.com; 89: © kcline/iStockphoto.com; 91: © KellyISP/iStockphoto.com; 96: © petrenkod/iStockphoto.com; 105: © tamara_kulikova/iStockphoto.com; 108: © YelenaYemchuk/iStockphoto.com; 110: © Marina Razumovskaya/iStockphoto.com; 118: © MaxCab/iStockphoto.com; 120: © Saaster/iStockphoto.com; 121: © LeeAnnWhite/iStockphoto.com; 124: © sf_foodphoto/iStockphoto.com; 126: © newzad/iStockphoto.com; 128: © helenecanada/iStockphoto.com; 129: © Alejandro Rivera/iStockphoto.com; 134: © sleddogtwo/iStockphoto.com; 136: © deepblue4you/iStockphoto.com; 144: © stu99/iStockphoto.com

Cover: © arinahabich/iStockphoto.com

index